D1567481

This book is dedicated to those who continue to remind
me that, "Anything can happen child. Anything can be."
In particular, to my mom and dad, L.Bo, Grandad Bollenback,
and of course, Ben. – *Meghan*

Book design by Lara Noel Key laranoel.com

CAPITAL AREA FOOD AND DRINK:
Western Loudoun
PRESERVED

BY MEGHAN BOLLENBACK & MARY LITTON

TABLE OF CONTENTS

INTRODUCTION

This project began over a glass of wine, as many great ideas do. We are two writers who shared a bottle of petit verdot inside the restored barn at Sunset Hills. As we looked out over the rows of grapevines that led straight to the silhouette of the Blue Ridge Mountains, we discussed our appreciation of good wine, farm-fresh meals, beautiful scenery, and a love of the written word. We shared a sense of gratitude for being able to enjoy these elements in rural Western Loudoun, just outside the busy suburbs of Washington, D.C. As our conversation continued, we realized we wanted to contribute in some way to preserve this section of land and its history for others to experience in the years to come.

We were excited by the opportunity to further explore Western Loudoun County in the form of great stories about food and drink, and, most importantly, about the people who grow and make them. Western Loudoun is a rural oasis that provides a barrier between urban development of the Washington, D.C. metro area and the Blue Ridge Mountains. It is a space that is steeped in history and serves as a visual reminder of Virginia's past. The small towns and villages in this direction offer a unique mix of farmland, 18th century homesteads, wineries, and historic villages that seem stopped in time. School groups visiting Western Loudoun can sit inside some of the state's first one-room school houses and visit grassy battlefields where they can actually picture a scene from the Civil War.

Western Loudoun is the heart of hunt country where gravel roads wind under canopies of towering trees, past rolling pastures protected by low-lying fog, and bordered by stone fences that stretch on for quiet miles. In the summer, the polo fields are electric green and in the fall, the soy crops turn a golden yellow that makes the landscape glow. You often see children jumping hay bales as the mountains become blue shadows with the sinking sun. In the winter, the red barns and black split rail fences create a sharp contrast to untouched white blankets of snow, while pillars of smoke rise from stone chimneys.

As the metropolitan D.C. area continues to evolve, there is growing pressure on this region to develop. While some development is necessary to keep towns economically sustainable, there is a question of how much development is too much? Do all of the open farmlands need to become planned communities, or can we somehow keep the land as is? These are some of the questions facing Western Loudoun, where the land and history are fiercely protected by a growing number of watchful caretakers.

These guardians quietly work to protect the ecosystems, the historic landscape, hallowed battlegrounds, and the food system. Their perceived motives for resisting change and development are often misunderstood. To them (and to us), the best way to protect against over-development is to share the stories of the land, its past use, and its potential for new things—be that grapevines, organic vegetables, or heritage animal breeds. They open the land for people to come and experience its beauty and its bounty, and to appreciate Western Loudoun for what it has always been. This small section of Northern Virginia is a tribute to our past and is the security for our future.

The stories of people and businesses reflected in this book are not an all-encompassing examination of all those who are working to preserve the rural nature of Western Loudoun, but they are a start. Our hope is that this book encourages others' conservation efforts to sustain and to appreciate the beauty and history that is Western Loudoun.

PURCELLVILLE

If you are looking for inspiration to begin your visit to Western Loudoun, we highly recommend using Purcellville as your first destination.

CENTRAL LANDING SPOT

Spending a Day in the Countryside

Purcellville is a delightful town centrally located with a mix of wineries, distilleries, boutiques and restaurants. It is the perfect location for beginning or ending your tour of the region. A Loudoun County visitor's center located in the historic train station provides maps and information about most tourist stops in the county. It is situated directly off of the famed Washington and Old Dominion (known as the W&OD by locals) bike trail, a 45-mile trail that starts in Purcellville, and meanders through the woods and farms of Western Loudoun and ends in Arlington County.

On Saturdays, you can find two farmers' markets in Purcellville, a great opportunity to pick up supplies for your outings. Additionally, it is home to a number of eclectic boutiques and antique stores in which shoppers can get lost for hours. Purcellville is quickly becoming known as the drink capital of Western Loudoun, and offers almost any liquid refreshment you could want.

LoCo Joe coffee shop is the community gathering space for Purcellville. The folks here are passionate about all things quality and local. Their small batch coffee and espresso beans and baked goods are sourced from Loudoun County or nearby farms and businesses. If you're lucky enough to be in Purcellville on a weekend in the spring, you can sit in the sunny living room of this house-turned-coffee shop and enjoy a cup of joe, tea, or local kombucha (from the tap!)

Dominion Tea Company operates from a tasting room in the historic downtown that allows visitors to sample nearly 100 different types of loose leaf teas. If you find something you like, you can order a flight of teas or simply purchase a pot to enjoy before heading out for your day trip.

Tomatoes at Potomac Vegetable Farms' Purcellville farm stand >

<< Summer blooms at Fields of Flowers, a U-pick flower farm in Purcellville

For those looking to enjoy a day of tasting stronger libations, Purcellville is the perfect spot to get your tour started. **Catoctin Creek Distillery** in a restored building downtown is the first distillery in Loudoun County since before prohibition and offers tours and a tasting room of award-winning, organic spirits. **Belly Love Brewing** offers craft beers on tap and a pet-friendly outdoor patio. **Corcoran Brewing Company** has twelve different house-made beers on tap and a busy entertainment schedule that includes live music and trivia. And for those looking to enjoy the Northern Virginia vineyards, Purcellville is the ideal place to start with the award-winning, bucolic Sunset Hills Winery.

In addition to great drinks, Purcellville offers a number of food options to help anchor your wine or beer tour. If you are looking for a lunch to go, **Butterfly Gourmet** offers a rotating menu of internationally inspired, gourmet lunches or **Monk's Barbecue** will hit the spot for a large, satisfying spread.

Market Burger makes an excellent start or end to your journey in Western Loudoun. Locally sourced ingredients make for decadent burgers, fries, and hand-dipped milkshakes. If you are looking for a little more upscale, **Magnolias at the Mill** and **West End Bistro** both offer fine dining and a great atmosphere that will help you relax after a day of tasting and exploring. 🍶

The iconic train station
in the heart of Purcellville ∨

Spiced Pumpkin Pie Shake

From Jason Lage at Market Burger
Serves 2 (or one if you're not keen on sharing!)

INGREDIENTS:

1 ½ cups vanilla bean
    ice cream

¾ cup whole milk

¼ cup pureed pumpkin
    sweetened with ½ teaspoon
    sugar (can substitute in ¼ cup
    of canned pumpkin pie filling)

Dash of pumpkin pie spice (omit
    if using pumpkin pie filling)

1 to 2 teaspoons crushed
    graham crackers

Drizzle of store-bought
    caramel sauce

DIRECTIONS:

In a high-powered blender, blend all ingredients from ice cream to pumpkin pie spice, if using, together. Add a little extra milk if you prefer a thinner shake. Divide the shake into two glasses (or just one) and top with crushed graham cracker and caramel sauce.

This is a fall favorite at Market Burger in Purcellville and bridges the gap between the warm, ice cream-filled summer months and the chilly, frosty winters! – *Rebecca Dudley*

Grapefruit Basil Martini

From Magnolias at the Mill
Serves 1

INGREDIENTS:

2 ounces Ketel One Vodka

1 ounce grapefruit juice

2 teaspoons simple syrup
(recipe below)

Fresh basil leaves

DIRECTIONS:

Mix vodka, grapefruit juice, and simple syrup in a cocktail shaker with ice. Shake well and pour into a martini glass. Garnish with a single basil leaf.

Optional: Wash and pat dry any leftover whole basil leaves. Freeze between pieces of paper towel and place in a plastic freezer bag. For future drinks, garnish with a frozen basil leaf.

Basic Simple Syrup

Makes 1 cup

INGREDIENTS:

1 cup sugar

1 cup water

DIRECTIONS:

Heat a small saucepan over medium-high heat and add the sugar and water. Stir occasionally for 10 to 15 minutes, until sugar has dissolved and the mixture comes to a boil.

Remove from heat and pour into a glass container that has a lid. Store in the refrigerator for up to one week. Use in coffee, tea, cocktails, or even as a topping on yogurt or oatmeal.

CATOCTIN CREEK DISTILLERY

Blazing Loudoun's Whisky Trail

120 W Main St
Purcellville, VA 20132

catoctincreekdistilling.com

When you first walk into Catoctin Creek Distillery in downtown Purcellville, you know there is something special going on there. It's not just their exquisitely designed tasting room with industrial tables and exposed brick, nor is it solely about their high quality spirits offered for tasting in flight form. Catoctin Creek is starting a movement to elevate our spirits on many levels.

Owners Scott and Becky Harris have always enjoyed good drinks. Becky is a chemical engineer with a background in production, and Scott previously worked with the government. "Twenty years as a government contractor taught me a great love of drinking," he jokes. Before opening the distillery, the duo would make a point to visit breweries, wineries and distilleries during their world travels. It was a trip to Bushmills distillery in Ireland that truly inspired Scott. He remembers looking around and thinking, "I want this."

After that trip, Scott went home and drew up a business plan that would wipe out all of their savings and make Becky the only unpaid employee of the distillery for a couple of years. Becky looked at the plan and figured that it was a good time to give it a try. "If it doesn't work out, we'll just do something else, that's just what you do," she remembers thinking. Six years later, they have exceeded their business plan goals and are continuing to grow. Fans of Catoctin Creek can be sure that the label distinction "distilled by" ensures the care given not only to the process but to the delightful end result.

Getting started in Loudoun County was not easy. While relaxed regulations were encouraging farm wineries and breweries throughout the county, the lingering stigma of prohibition and difficult zoning regulations left a dearth in the county's spirits. Scott and Becky went before the state legislature three times, finding success twice to change regulations that would help Catoctin Creek. Success comes in small changes. As Scott says, they were "taking bites of the apple" instead of pushing for huge regulatory changes.

< Becky Harris checks the stills for the day's whisky batch

<< Whisky barrels line the distillery walls at Catoctin Creek Distillery

Both Scott and Becky concur that the timing and location for a Loudoun distillery are perfect. There has been a lingering mindset that wine and beer are more acceptable than spirits, but that mindset is quickly changing thanks to those in their 20s and 30s. "The millennial generation is much more comfortable and excited about it," Becky says. "They want to go out and taste it and drink cocktails."

In addition to the new trend toward spirits, Loudoun County is a great location for a distillery since it is on the outskirts of the district. "D.C. is a foodie town with a young demographic and a lot of culture," Scott says. He thinks that it is the marriage of geography and the local food movement that have made Catoctin Creek successful so quickly.

The couple strive to be more than just local. Catoctin Creek Distillery is one of the only distilleries in the nation to be certified organic and kosher. There were several reasons they decided to be organic, including wanting to be historically accurate. The duo uses recipes from the turn of the 20th century. Being organic helps them stay more true to a whisky made in 1910 because herbicides weren't used then. Being organic also makes for a better tasting spirit.

"If you take a sample right off the still, it's just clean and beautiful right as it is," says Scott. A non-organic grain would have to be aged in a barrel to remove some of the off-tastes such as petroleum. "Being organic is one of the reasons we can make a whisky that is relatively young and tastes really nice," continues Scott. Finally, being organic helps with sustainability and allows Catoctin Creek to better care for farmers. The distillery is creating a demand for organic grains in the area. These are a higher value crop, and according to the couple, help encourage farmers to turn their fields over to organic grain.

< The daily specials
in the tasting room

Catoctin Creek's commitment to sustainability goes further than just using organic products. When renovating an old building, they added solar panels to produce 80 percent of their electricity. Additionally, they have a zero waste production process by giving mash to local farmers to use as livestock feed, and any undrinkable alcohol is sent to a state refinery and turned into ethanol for cars. ૐ

A flight of gin and whisky cocktails in the tasting room >

Hot Buttered Rye

Developed by Chad Robinson for the Edible D.C. Spirits Festival
Serves 1

INGREDIENTS:
1 tablespoon softened butter

1 tablespoon brown sugar

⅛ teaspoon of cinnamon

⅛ teaspoon of nutmeg

⅛ teaspoon of allspice

⅛ teaspoon of clove

⅛ teaspoon of ginger

¾ cup boiling water

1 ounce Catoctin Creek
   Roundstone Rye

DIRECTIONS:
In a mug or cocktail shaker, mix soft butter, brown sugar, and spices together thoroughly to form a batter. Add boiling water to your batter and stir well until a frothy top forms. Stir in your rye and garnish with nutmeg or a cinnamon stick.

Roundstone Rye Chocolate Bundt Cake

From Meghan Bollenback, adapted from Dorie Greenspan
Serves 8 to 12

INGREDIENTS:

2 sticks, plus 1 tablespoon unsalted butter, softened

2 cups, plus 2 tablespoons all purpose flour

1 cup water

¼ cup instant coffee or espresso powder

2 tablespoons unsweetened cocoa powder

1 cup plus 1 teaspoon Catoctin Creek's Roundstone Rye whisky

½ teaspoon kosher salt

5 ounces bittersweet or unsweetened chocolate (recommend using 70 to 80 percent high-quality dark chocolate, such as Valrhona)

2 cups granulated sugar

3 large eggs

1 tablespoon vanilla extract

1 teaspoon baking soda

Powdered sugar

DIRECTIONS:

Preheat oven to 325°F. Thoroughly grease a bundt pan with one tablespoon butter and then sprinkle with 2 tablespoons flour.

Boil a cup of water in a teapot or in a pot on the stove. While that heats, put the instant coffee and cocoa powder into a two-cup glass liquid measuring cup. Add enough boiling water to come up to the one cup measuring line. Stir until the powders dissolve, then add the whisky and salt. Let cool.

While the liquid cools, sift flour into a medium bowl and set aside. Then, melt the chocolate in a double boiler on the stovetop (place chocolate in a pan that's resting on a pot filled with simmering water and stir occasionally until melted), or in a microwave. If using the microwave, use a glass or ceramic bowl and heat for 1 minute at 50% power. Stir, and then continue this process at 20-second intervals until chocolate is melted.

In a large bowl, beat the two sticks of butter with an electric mixer on medium until light and fluffy, about two minutes. Add the sugar and beat until combined. Then, add eggs one by one, beating well after each new egg. Add the vanilla, baking soda, and melted chocolate. Scrape down the sides of the bowl and beat until combined for about 30 seconds to one minute.

With the mixer on low, add a third of the whisky/cocoa mixture to the bowl. After it is mixed in, add in half of the sifted flour and beat until just combined. Scrape down sides, and then repeat the process. End by adding in the final third of the whisky/cocoa mixture. Make sure it is combined, but do not over mix. It's fine if the mixture appears a little soupy.

Pour into the prepared bundt pan and bake for 60 to 75 minutes, until a toothpick inserted into the middle comes out mostly clean. Remove from the oven and let cool for 30 to 35 minutes in the pan. Then, flip over onto a plate or cutting board and gently shake to release the cake. Drizzle a teaspoon of extra whisky on top. If serving the next day, lightly cover and leave on the countertop overnight. Before serving, sprinkle the cake with a little powdered sugar.

This cake is delicious out of the oven but tastes even better on the second or third day as the whisky has time to mellow after baking. While this calls for a good amount of whisky, do not reduce—you'll lose the whisky flavor to the chocolate if you do. – *Meghan Bollenback*

SUNSET HILLS

From Grower to Winery; How the Changing Laws Support a Changing Business

On any given Saturday at Sunset Hills Vineyard, it's not unusual to see parents and their children run and play on the expansive fields that border the vineyards. At the same time, bachelorette parties may be enjoying a sip of rosé or the house-made Wine-a-Ritas, and the casual wine connoisseur may thoughtfully take notes on a tasting list to remember the scents and flavors noticed in each pour.

38295 Fremont Overlook Ln
Purcellville, VA 20132

sunsethillsvineyard.com

Somehow, Sunset Hills seems to have mastered the art of catering to a wide variety of visitors without sacrificing on quality in any regard—be that location, wine, or service. It is consistently recognized as one of the most beautiful wineries to visit in Western Loudoun, thanks in part to its iconic, restored Amish barn. Built in 1878, and featuring a rooster weathervane atop it and wrap-around porch, this is one of the most highly awarded Northern Virginia wineries.

The vineyard, located two miles outside of downtown Purcellville, began as an independent grower, or more simply, a grape farm. Mike and Diane Canney planted the first crop of grapes in 1999. Over the next 9 years, they expanded their farmland to 20 acres and eventually decided to transition into the winery business. As of 2015, they have 75 acres under vine. One of the major factors that led to this business model change was the support of farm wineries from the Virginia and Loudoun County governments. State legislative changes that were passed in 1980 allowed farmers to grow grapes and operate a winery on their land for tourism and business purposes. This essentially opened the door to agritourism in the form of wineries.

Inside Sunset Hills'
tasting room >

<< The barn at Sunset Hills
dates back to the 1870s

Overall, the farm winery model has been widely adopted and supported across the state largely due to the increase in tourism and money that it brings to the region. In 1980, there were only 20 wineries in Virginia. Three decades later, that number has surpassed 220, and most of that growth has happened since the early 2000s. Loudoun County alone has over 40 wineries. Additionally, Visit Loudoun, a local tourism organization, has increasingly marketed the western area of the county as a wine destination and branded it as "D.C.'s Wine Country."

The impact that both the state and county legislatures and marketing changes have had on Sunset Hills is not lost on its winemaker, Nate Walsh. He joined the vineyard in 2009 after spending time making wine in Charlottesville, Virginia as well as in Oregon and New Zealand. Walsh thinks that Virginia's "small but growing [wine industry] still has a lot to prove and establish." He happily admits that it has improved by leaps and bounds over the past decade that he has been in the state, but gets serious when he thinks about what needs to be done to elevate the county and state's overall image as a winemaking region.

"The tourism [for Western Loudoun] is so good because we're so close to D.C. That's really great for the wineries. But it's really important, in my opinion, to plant Virginia vineyards in the right place and make quality wine. There were a number of years in Western Loudoun where you could really sell anything because people would buy it. But, now that's changing. The cream will have to rise to the top to stay afloat."

Walsh says that the goal at Sunset Hills is "to provide really interesting wines and the best wines in the area," while also making as little of a negative impact on the environment as possible. He and the Canneys pay special attention to their wine club members and plan to begin distributing over the next year or two, ideally into D.C. and other neighboring cities.

Walsh feels one thing that may help their wines is the priority they place on keeping the overall ecosystem thriving while minimizing the environmental impact of the farm. He happily explains that they use Virginia sunshine twice at Sunset Hills; once to grow the grapes on the vines, and again to power their operations and tasting room areas through solar power. They don't use herbicides on their grapes, and pesticides are used at an absolute minimum.

< Sunset Hills has won
numerous awards for its wines

"We want to preserve property by planting on it. We're always interested in new land, but don't want to develop it—just plant," he says.

When asked about his feelings on Virginia's marketing of viognier as the 'state's grape', Walsh vehemently states that he is pro-viognier. He knows other growers in Western Loudoun and beyond may not feel the same way due to it being one of the most difficult and temperamental grapes to grow, but he truly believes that it is one of the highest quality and expressive white wine grapes that Virginia can support. It all comes back to his original sentiment—location is key.

"I think some growers feel frustrated by the grape in part due to the rapid growth of the industry and the demand for more wine. They see an open field and say, 'Let's plant viognier there,' and then it's not until five years later that they realize it doesn't work there. We've made that mistake. Last year we ripped out half an acre because it wasn't a match for that spot," he admits.

Still, Walsh remains optimistic and thinks it can and will be a sustainable grape for the state. Whether he's right, only time will tell, as Loudoun County and Virginia wines as a whole need time to simply age and improve. 🍇

VIOGNIER — VIRGINIA'S GRAPE?

Viognier is a varietal from the Rhône region of France that many Virginia wineries have adopted as one of their flagship grapes, for better or for worse. It can grow in certain parts of the state, but it is fickle, as it needs a higher vigor, which means it requires a more aggressive nutrient program and less water.

Nate Walsh uses fish oil and seaweed sprays to increase the nitrogen in viognier grapes at Sunset Hills. Before he (and many other growers and winemakers) plants any varietal, he brings in geologists to inspect and identify by block the types of soils, nutrients, and moisture levels so that he knows which grapes to match to each block in their land.

A Cheeseboard, Perfect for a Picnic

From Meghan Bollenback
Serves 10 for a light lunch or appetizer

INGREDIENTS:

Cheeses:

8 ounces of a semi-firm or medium cheese
    such as Brie, Feta, or Swiss

8 ounces of a soft cheese
    such as Gorgonzola or Chèvre

8 ounces of a hard cheese such as
    Gouda, Parmesan Reggiano, or Asiago

Meats:

8 ounces sliced prosciutto

8 ounces sliced Genoa salami

Fruits, Nuts, and Other Snacks:

1 pound seedless green or red grapes

1 jar Kalamata olives, removed from brine

1 jar gherkins, removed from brine

12 ounces lightly salted mixed nuts

Spreads:

1 jar fig or berry jam

1 jar onion or pepper jelly

Breads and Crackers:

1 to 2 long French baguettes,
    sliced into 1-inch wide pieces

1 pack of water crackers

1 pack of thin, crunchy breadsticks

DIRECTIONS:

If taking to a picnic, pack the cheeses (wrap first in parchment and a Ziploc bag), meats, fruit, olives, and gherkins in a cooler lightly filled with ice. Pack the spreads, nuts, breads, and crackers in a bag. Spread everything out across a blanket and enjoy—remember to bring napkins!

If serving at home, place the cheeses, meats, snacks, and crackers onto various platters and place serving utensils and toothpicks by each item. Or, line a table with parchment and place directly onto the paper.

Building a cheeseboard is an experiment in creativity and texture. This recipe is meant to be a guide—feel free to use your favorite types of cheese, meat, jams, fruits, nuts, and crunchy breads or crackers. Just remember to enjoy with a bottle or two of Sunset Hills wine, ideally on a sunny spring or summer day. *– Meghan Bollenback*

LOCO JOE

The LoCo Joe coffee shop is the community gathering space for Purcellville that constantly fills with people who are passionate about all things quality and local. The shop's coffee and baked goods are sourced from Loudoun County or nearby regional farms and businesses. If you're lucky enough to visit Purcellville on a weekend in the spring, you can sit in the sunny living room of this house-turned-coffee shop and enjoy a cup of joe, tea, or local kombucha (from the tap!). ☕

550 E Main St
Purcellville, VA 20132

locojoecoffee.com

Japanese Iced Coffee

From LoCo Joe
Serves 1

INGREDIENTS:

Ice

1 ½ cups chilled, brewed coffee (dark or espresso roast is highly suggested)

2 tablespoons vanilla simple syrup (recipe below)

1 to 2 tablespoons half-and-half

DIRECTIONS:

Fill a large cup (one that can hold at least 16 ounces) with ice. Add coffee until three-quarters of the way full and then drizzle in the vanilla simple syrup. Top off with a tablespoon or two of half-and-half, using more if you want a creamier concoction.

Vanilla Simple Syrup

Makes 1 cup

INGREDIENTS:

1 cup sugar

1 cup water

1 vanilla bean

DIRECTIONS:

Heat a small saucepan over medium-high heat and add the sugar and water. Slice vanilla bean down the center on one side (do not cut all the way through if you can help it) and scrape out the black seeds. Add the seeds and pod to the liquid mixture.

Heat and stir occasionally for 10 to 15 minutes, until sugar has dissolved and the mixture comes to a boil.

Remove from heat and pour into a glass container that has a lid. Store in the refrigerator for up to one week. Use in coffee, tea, cocktails, or even as a topping on yogurt or oatmeal.

USING FOOD AS MEDICINE

Elaine Boland is a strong advocate of using nutrition as medicine. And, lucky for those in the D.C. metro area that she is the owner of Fields of Athenry, a farm in Purcellville that raises sheep, beef, poultry, and waterfowl, and sells them on-site at the farm and nationally.

38082 Snickersville Turnpike
Purcellville, VA 20132

fieldsofathenryfarm.com

One morning, we are invited to sit around their large kitchen table and listen to Elaine, Bernadette, and Mary Teresa Boland tell the story of how they came to be practitioners of nutrient-dense, whole-animal foods, and bone broths. Their story begins in the early 2000s when Elaine noticed something did not seem quite right with her second youngest daughter, Bernadette. Elaine recalls that Bernadette suddenly gained a substantial amount of weight, often felt fatigued, and was no longer able to stay balanced atop her horse. "Something's wrong with a child when she just can't get up and go. That's when I really knew," Elaine explains.

Elaine and her family spent years trying to determine the cause of Bernadette's issues. As they sought answers, Elaine decided she would be proactive with her daughter's health, so she began to research the link between nutrition and health. She found the teachings of Weston A. Price, an early 20th century dentist and researcher who was a proponent of the connection between nutrition and physical health. Soon after that, her research led her to find *Nourishing Traditions*, a cookbook by Sally Fallon and Mary G. Enig, Ph.D., two enthusiastic supporters of Price. Elaine chose to use it as a guide.

The book inspired her to raise her animals at Fields of Athenry in a holistic manner that allows them to thrive while alive in order to reap their full nutritional value after slaughter. This "whole-animal" approach to farming, which she carries on today, includes certain tenets such as letting babies stay with their mothers and interact naturally with them after birth, practicing intensive rotational grazing methods, and letting them use their natural instincts to ward off illness (something that is inhibited when animals are confined). Hormones and chemicals are not used on the animals, nor are antibiotics unless in extreme life-or-death situations.

< Sheep at Fields of Athenry use a rotational grazing method

<< The sign from the road as you pull into Fields of Athenry

In the kitchen, Elaine began to experiment with bone broths and other nutrient-dense foods. It took her two years to develop a recipe for her broth that she now sells in the farm store on property and ships nationally. "I had to make it taste really, really good, or else they [her daughters and husband] wouldn't eat it," she laughingly divulges. Other items such as raw milk and cheeses, organ meats, vegetables and fruits became the norm in her household, while sugar and grains were tossed out.

The typical American family likely would have revolted against such a drastic change in eating habits, but the Boland family's love for one another, interest in seeing Bernadette healthy again, and responsibilities as farmers led the family of seven to fully adopt the new diet. Mary Teresa, who was a college student at the time, admits to turning into a "food snob" and took her mom's offerings back to school because the food was much tastier than the typical dining hall fare.

Bernadette was eventually diagnosed with Cushing's disease, an endocrine disorder that leads to high levels of cortisol in the body. As part of Bernadette's treatment plan, Elaine supplements her diet with bone broths and even named one after her daughter. Bernadette's Broth is now one of the most popular items sold by Fields of Athenry.

As for Elaine, she continues to make and sell broths, meats, offal, and other nutrient-dense foods to a growing list of patrons and constantly restocks the freezers at her farm store. She has become a leader for others wanting to learn how to use nutrition to improve their physical health. 🐾

< The shelves are stocked
with goods to sell in the farm store

Favorite Lamb Recipe

From Elaine Boland at Fields of Athenry
Serves 6 to 8

INGREDIENTS:

1 tablespoon salted
 Amish butter*

1 tablespoon pork lard

1 handful each of fresh
 rosemary, thyme, and
 oregano, chopped

2 to 3 teaspoons
 Premier Pink Salt*

2 to 3 teaspoons
 Mom's Seasoning*

2 ½ pounds Fields of Athenry
 lamb loin roast, butterflied
 leg of lamb or top round

1 large diced yellow onion

¾ cup Harvey's Bristol
 Cream sherry

1 pound sliced button
 mushrooms

*Amish butter, Premier Pink
Salt and Mom's Seasoning can be
purchased at the Fields of Athenry
market at the farm. If you can't
make it to Purcellville, you can
substitute any farm-fresh butter
available, sea salt, and your
favorite meat-seasoning blend.*

DIRECTIONS:

Preheat convection oven to 350°F.

In heavy skillet, melt slab of Amish butter and pork lard over medium-high heat. Add in the rosemary, thyme, oregano, Premier Pink Salt, and Mom's Seasoning and let cook for about one minute, until fragrant.

Add the lamb to the pan and sear for a couple minutes until it deepens in color (do not touch the lamb while it sears!). Then, flip lamb over and sear the other side. Repeat until all sides are seared evenly. Remove lamb from the pan and place it onto a shallow baking pan. Top with the herbs and seasonings and then place in the oven for 20 to 30 minutes. Remove when the lamb's center temperature reaches 125°F (for medium rare) or 130–135°F (for medium).

While lamb cooks, make a gravy. Keep the skillet set to medium heat. Add onions and the Harvey's Bristol Cream sherry to the hot skillet and sauté for five to eight minutes. Add mushrooms and sauté for another three to five minutes until they have browned.

Once the lamb is cooked through, remove from the oven and let rest for at least five minutes. When ready to serve, slice into medallions, place onto a platter and drizzle with the gravy from the skillet.

Serve with peas and carrots, wild rice and apples, or a fresh garden salad, and you have a perfect lamb dinner!

FOA Fresh Chicken Soup

From Elaine Boland at Fields of Athenry
Serves 4

INGREDIENTS:

2 tablespoons olive oil

4 Fields of Athenry boneless skinless chicken breasts cut into bite-sized pieces

1 teaspoon fresh basil

1 teaspoon minced garlic

1 teaspoon oregano

1 ½ teaspoon kosher salt

½ teaspoon black pepper

1 small chopped onion

3 diced carrots

2 thinly sliced zucchini

2 diced tomatoes

1 (32-ounce) container of Fields of Athenry Liquid Gold Chicken Stock

6 ounces grated Fields of Athenry Raw Milk Sharp Cheddar Cheese

Fresh parsley

DIRECTIONS:

In a large Dutch oven, heat olive oil over medium-high heat. Add chicken pieces, basil, minced garlic, oregano and salt and pepper to taste and cook for 10 minutes, stirring frequently. Add onion and carrots, and cook for 6 to 8 minutes. Stir in zucchini, diced tomatoes, and chicken stock. Bring to a boil and then reduce heat and simmer, uncovered, for 30 minutes.

Transfer the soup to serving bowls and top with grated cheddar and snips of parsley.

Broths are a wonderful component to one's weekly diet—they are a natural glucosamine for our joints and old knees. There are many ways one can incorporate broths. I love sipping on them like a cup of coffee or tea in the morning—it's an instant breakfast and filling, too. Or, use broth when cooking rice instead of water. It also makes a delicious gravy or can be used when sautéing vegetables. One can quickly turn the broths into a meal, stretching the family budget to go a long way. This soup is one of my favorite recipes I developed to get my girls crazy about broth! – *Elaine Boland*

LEESBURG

Leesburg is the county seat of Loudoun and serves as a gateway to the more rural parts of the county. The charming, quaint downtown has a long history that spans over three centuries and is home to a vibrant and eclectic mix of boutiques, crafters, and restaurants.

TUSKIES RESTAURANTS

Loudoun is One Big Family

Like a respected patriarch at the head of the table, Tuscarora Mill sits in the center of downtown Leesburg. Opened in 1985, and located in a historic mill that has been transformed into a rustic modern dining room, it became the first of five restaurants the Tuskies Group would start. With its energetic vibe and consistently good food, Tuscarora Mill is one of the defining restaurants and event spaces of Western Loudoun.

203 Harrison St SE
Leesburg, VA 20175

tuskies.com

Over the years, owner Kevin Malone has collected a lot of wisdom, but if there is one thing he understands best, it's people. "This is a people business," he explains, "and we want our people to be happy." As a young bartender with an interest in psychology, Malone was drawn to the restaurant industry where he was able to combine his people skills with his business acumen. The result is a loyal network of employees and customers to support his growing number of establishments. At the center of this network is head chef Patrick Dinh, who has been at Tuscarora for more than 25 years and is now part owner of the Tuskies Group's pizza restaurant, Fireworks.

Together, Malone and Dinh have created a structure of loyalty and upward mobility for their 300 employees. They are proud to point out that they have 18 employees who have tenure of two decades or more. Two of their current managers and head bread baker started as dishwashers. "Our employees are the most important thing," says Malone. "We support our employees and want to see them grow in their careers." Chef Dinh attributes much of their culinary success to his staff. "I have four people who have 20 plus years. We can be working right next to each other and not have to say a thing—we already know what the other is doing."

In addition to knowing their employees, having an understanding of their customer base has also helped with their success. "We do a lot of research and development," Malone says, referring to his most recent outing where he hired a bus to take nine employees up to a restaurant in Baltimore. "I always choose a place where I think I can learn something." This type of research has paid off well. Indeed, his vision for Fireworks Pizza, with its casual atmosphere and wood fired specialties, was inspired by a trip to American Flatbread in Vermont. And while he enjoys trying new things, it always goes back to the customers. "You have to have the smarts to say that while this is what we think we might want, this is not what our customers want, and you go back and revise," says Malone. Dinh adds, "We bend over backwards for our customers."

From Malone's perspective, everyone is a potential customer. That is why, decades ago, he started buying local before the phrase "farm-to-table" was even coined. He recognizes the importance of supporting other local businesses, and in Western Loudoun, this includes the farmers. Not only does Malone have access to fresh, high-quality ingredients, but he says that many of the farmers in the area are good customers.

<< Tuscarora Mill is located in an old grain mill in the heart of downtown Leesburg

In addition to supporting local farmers, Tuskies Group also began a campaign to help the wine industry. They created a tourist map of their favorite wineries that is now distributed all over Loudoun County including the Visitor's Center. Supporting the wineries benefits not only the region but also directs wine tourists to his restaurants. While it makes for good business, Malone appreciates the value of supporting these other ventures. "Our kids are lucky to grow up in a community where they can drive past farms and vineyards instead of strip malls," he says.

Building interpersonal business relationships with employees and customers is not easy. Malone and Dinh admit that it is really hard work to get to know everyone on a deeper level, but they are committed to making the time and taking interest. "This is our life," they explain. The hard work does pay off. One of the first couples to have their wedding reception at Tuscarora just returned to host their daughter's wedding reception. "We are very much a part of the community," explains Dinh. "Long-time Loudouners come here all the time, not because they don't have other choices, but this is where they choose to go." ❧

< The bar at Tuskies
is a local favorite

Fried Green Tomato Salad with Burrata, Basil and Tomato-Dill Vinaigrette

From Executive Chef Patrick Dinh at Tuscarora Mill
Serves 4

INGREDIENTS:

1 cup fresh diced tomatoes

¾ cup tomato juice

½ cup white wine vinegar, preferably champagne

2 finely diced shallots

1 teaspoon minced garlic

2 tablespoons minced fresh dill

1 tablespoon steak seasoning

¾ cup extra virgin olive oil

3 medium green tomatoes

2 cups flour seasoned with salt and pepper

2 eggs

¼ cup buttermilk or regular milk

8 ounces burrata cheese

Canola or vegetable oil for frying

4 ounces baby arugula

Fresh basil leaves

DIRECTIONS:

Mix diced tomatoes, tomato juice, white wine vinegar, shallots, garlic, dill, and steak seasoning in mixing bowl. While whisking, slowly add the olive oil until combined. Set aside.

In a separate bowl, whisk together the two eggs and buttermilk or milk until combined. Set aside.

Slice green tomatoes into ¼-inch slices, should make about eight. Dredge both sides of the tomato slices in the seasoned flour followed by the egg and milk mixture. Once well coated, return to the seasoned flour and dredge again. Place coated tomato slices onto a plate.

In a 12-inch skillet, pour enough oil to cover ¼-inch. Heat until oil begins to shimmer, about 350°F. Carefully place dredged tomato slices into oil and fry two minutes each side. Drain on paper towels.

Arrange arugula on plate and top with slices of fried green tomatoes. Separate burrata into four sections and then divide each section into two additional slices to place on top of each slice of tomato. Dress with the tomato-dill vinaigrette and sprinkle with torn basil leaves.

Serve immediately.

Gulf Shrimp and Grits

From Executive Chef Patrick Dinh at Tuscarora Mill
Serves 4

INGREDIENTS:

1 cup heavy cream

1 cup water

Salt and black pepper to taste

½ cup stone-ground grits

¼ pound Asiago cheese

Dash of truffle oil

½ cup diced country ham

1 peeled and finely diced shallot

2 tablespoons finely chopped garlic

24–28 large raw shrimp, peeled and deveined

4 ounces Madeira wine

½ pound of fresh spinach

½ cup diced tomatoes

½ stick unsalted butter

DIRECTIONS:

In a large saucepan over medium-high heat, combine cream and water. Bring to a gentle boil. Add salt and pepper. Slowly add all of the grits, stirring constantly so that the grits do not settle to the bottom and scorch.

Reduce heat to medium-low. Cook for 30 minutes or until grits are tender, stirring occasionally and being careful not to scorch the mixture. The grits should have absorbed all of the liquid and become soft. They should be moist, not dry, with the same consistency as oatmeal. If the grits become too thick, add warm stock or water to thin. When done, add cheese and truffle oil. Stir. Remove from heat and cover to keep warm.

Season shrimp with salt and pepper; set aside.

In a large frying pan over medium-high heat, cook country ham until brown but not crisp. Add shallots and garlic and stir for 1 minute until fragrant. Add shrimp, sauté 5 minutes. Deglaze pan with Madeira. Add tomatoes and spinach and continue to cook until spinach is wilted and shrimp is fully pink. Lower heat to medium-low and add butter. Swirl to emulsify. Add salt and pepper to taste. Serve over grits.

Maple Glazed Sea Scallops with Farro and Butternut Squash

From Executive Chef Patrick Dinh at Tuscarora Mill
Serves 4

INGREDIENTS:

1 cup farro

5 tablespoons vegetable oil, divided

3 cups coarsely diced (¾ inch cubes) butternut squash

¼ cup maple syrup

1 teaspoon ketchup

1 teaspoon BBQ sauce

4 tablespoons unsalted butter

½ cup finely diced onions

½ cup finely diced carrots

½ cup finely diced celery

1 teaspoon chopped garlic

2 pounds of large sea scallops, abductor muscle removed

½ cup toasted pecan pieces

Salt and pepper

DIRECTIONS:

Preheat oven to 425°F.

Cook farro in one quart of salted boiling water until tender, about 20 minutes. Drain, rinse, and set aside.

Toss the diced butternut squash in a mixing bowl with about three tablespoons of vegetable oil, plus salt and pepper. Place on a baking sheet large enough to hold them in a single layer and put the pan in oven. Roast for about 25 minutes or until tender, using a metal spatula to turn and shake them after 12 minutes so they cook evenly.

Mix maple syrup, ketchup, and BBQ sauce together, set aside.

Sauté the diced onions, carrots, celery, and chopped garlic in the butter in a nonstick skillet. When the vegetables are tender add the cooked farro and sauté together, season with salt and pepper. Keep warm.

Completely dry the scallops by patting with paper towels and then season with salt and pepper on one side. Heat the remaining vegetable oil in a large, very hot skillet. Working in two batches, carefully place scallops about one inch apart and sear for two minutes per side. Repeat with second batch.

Place the hot farro pilaf in the center of a serving dish and flank the pilaf with small mounds of roasted butternut squash. Place the hot scallops on top of the pilaf. Smear the maple glaze on the scallops with the back of a spoon, then drizzle the extra glaze around the plate. Sprinkle the plate with toasted pecans.

Tuskie's Waldorf Salad with Champagne Vinaigrette

From Executive Chef Patrick Dinh at Tuscarora Mill
Serves 4

INGREDIENTS:

For the spiced walnuts:

2 cups chopped walnuts

¾ cup powdered sugar

1 teaspoon cayenne powder

1 teaspoon curry powder

1 teaspoon paprika

1 teaspoon allspice

2 teaspoons salt

For the champagne vinaigrette:

½ cup champagne vinegar

2 teaspoons finely
   chopped garlic

¼ cup finely chopped shallots

¼ cup Dijon mustard

2 tablespoons chopped parsley

1 cup canola oil

1 cup extra virgin olive oil

Salt and pepper, to taste

For salad:

4 chicken breasts,
   about 6 ounces each

8 ounces Cambozola cheese
   (can substitute with
   Gorgonzola)

1 Asian pear, peeled

2 stalks of celery

1 cup seedless grapes

8 ounces of baby greens

2 ripe tomatoes, sliced into
   12 round slices for garnish

Salt and pepper, to taste

DIRECTIONS:

Preheat oven to 400°F. Also, prepare and preheat your grill or grill pan.

Place the nuts in a colander and rinse evenly under hot running water for about one minute while actively stirring. Drain and place in a mixing bowl. Coat the nuts liberally with powdered sugar and spices and arrange evenly on a baking sheet that has been lined with parchment paper and sprayed with nonstick spray (such as Pam). Bake for about 10 minutes, turning the nuts over halfway through to ensure even cooking. When the nuts are toasted and dry, remove and let cool. They'll harden at room temperature.

Place vinegar, garlic, shallots, Dijon mustard, parsley, salt, and pepper in a mixing bowl and mix with a whisk. Slowly add the canola and olive oil a couple tablespoons at a time until all of it is emulsified and well combined. Place in refrigerator.

Grill the chicken breasts until cooked through, about 5 to 6 minutes per side. Let rest for 3 minutes and then slice into fork-friendly pieces. While chicken cooks and rests, cut Cambozola into chunks and slice the Asian pear into bite-sized chunks. Slice celery thinly on a bias, about ⅛ inch thick. Slice grapes in half.

In a mixing bowl, toss the chicken, celery, pears, grapes, spiced walnuts, and Cambozola with ¼ cup champagne vinaigrette.

Separately, toss the mixed greens with another ¼ cup of champagne vinaigrette. Place the greens on the bottom of a large serving platter or divide onto four large individual plates. Divide the mixture on top of the greens. Garnish with sliced tomatoes. Store remaining vinaigrette in a tightly sealed jar for up to a week.

Smokey Blue Pizza

From Fireworks Pizza
Serves 4

INGREDIENTS:

½ pound bacon

1 small sliced Vidalia onion

10 ounces pizza dough
(raw dough is available
for purchase at Fireworks)

½ cup tomato sauce

1 cup shredded
pizza blend cheese

4 ounces crumbled
Gorgonzola cheese

Fresh rosemary

¼ cup store-bought
balsamic vinegar glaze

DIRECTIONS:

Heat a large pan to medium-high heat. Chop bacon, add to pan, and cook until darkened in color and slightly crispy. Reduce heat to medium, then remove bacon and rest on a plate that has been lined with a paper towel (do not drain the grease yet). Add Vidalia onion slices into the pan and sauté until translucent, 6 to 8 minutes.

While bacon and onions cook, preheat oven to 375°F. Place pizza stone or large baking sheet in the oven to warm.

On a well-floured cutting board that can be used to transport the pizza, roll out dough to about 14 inches in diameter.

Spread tomato sauce over the dough leaving a half-inch edge for the crust. Spread half of the shredded cheese over the pizza. Sprinkle crumbled bacon, onions, rosemary and Gorgonzola on top. Cover with the remaining shredded blend.

Transfer the loaded pizza onto the preheated stone or baking sheet. Bake for 15 to 20 minutes, until crust is blistered and golden brown. Lift pizza edge to view the underside of the center of the pie to ensure it's completely cooked. Once pizza is fully cooked, cut into slices. Drizzle the balsamic glaze in a circular motion moving from the center of the pie to the edge.

Butterscotch Bread Pudding

From South Street Under
Serves 8

INGREDIENTS:

One loaf French bread,
   or any firm textured bread

4 eggs

1 cup plus 3 tablespoons sugar,
   divided

2 cups heavy cream

2 cups half & half

⅓ cup butterscotch schnapps

¼ cup softened unsalted butter

1 cup butterscotch chips

Toppings:
Store-bought whipped cream
Store-bought caramel sauce

DIRECTIONS:

Dice the bread into half-inch cubes. Combine eggs, 1 cup of sugar, cream, half & half, and schnapps in a large bowl and stir well to form custard. Add the bread cubes to the custard and stir to coat. Allow to sit and absorb the custard, stirring occasionally. This may take as little as 30 minutes if bread is fresh or up to one hour if bread is slightly stale.

While bread is soaking, preheat oven to 350°F. Rub a three-quart shallow baking dish generously with the softened butter. Sprinkle with 3 tablespoons sugar and tap out any excess.

Stir the butterscotch chips into the bread mixture and pour into prepared pan. Smooth out the top, but note that it will be a little rough! Bake approximately one hour, or until nicely browned. Serve warm with whipped cream and warm caramel sauce.

DOWNTOWN LEESBURG

The Devine Touch

19 W Market St
Leesburg, VA 20175

tallyholeesburg.com

There is something cosmic about Don Devine, a self-professed "downtown food and entertainment advocate" for Leesburg. His charming smile and energetic persona exude confidence—the kind of guy engaged in things that tend to work out. Maybe it comes from the comfort of being born and raised in a prominent Loudoun County family. This is the place where he, too, chose to raise his own family, and where he is now proudly in business with his children. Whatever the source of his inner reserve of confidence, it spills over into his life's work of buying and leasing out buildings in downtown Leesburg. He gives downtown Leesburg "a Devine touch."

Devine's passion for preserving his hometown is evident through his purchase of buildings where he is always mindful of protecting the historic exteriors while changing the interiors. He considers himself a strange mix of part developer and part preservationist as he places modern, locally owned businesses in old, preserved buildings. "I'm an artist and buildings are my medium," he explains. He loves the variety of architecture that makes up Leesburg—a testament to the town's evolution and history. Interested in preserving much more than just the typical colonial structures, Devine enjoys the eclectic mix of periods yielding a living museum of architecture. He thinks that residents and visitors find it more interesting when you have a downtown mixed with art deco, colonial, modern, and turn of the century buildings.

While preserving the town's history, flexibility has always been a key to Devine's business success. He feels that loyalty to a tenant is important as economics ebb and flow. His ability to work with his tenants during downturns has helped them stay loyal to him during upturns, and this helps keep local owners in the downtown buildings instead of turning them over to developers.

Devine points out the historical details of a building in downtown Leesburg. >

<< The Tally Ho is the "sexiest building" in Leesburg according to Don Devine

Upon meeting us, Devine is eager to show off the beauty of this town. Before we have time to gather our things, we are off on a tour like a shot out of a cannon. As he leads us from King Street through an alley and down the side streets, traffic stops for him, people call out their hellos as we disappear through the front door of an old house. Inside, we are split between two restaurants—Windy City Red Hots and Blue Mountain Café. We glide through kitchens, out a side door and back through an alley that used to be a barn. ("Have you ever seen a barn door this old before?" asks Devine.) We now find ourselves at the back stairs of an old house containing some of the oldest preserved photographs in Loudoun County. (We had no idea Hessian soldiers hired by the British lived in captivity above the tavern.) Next, we are down in front of a warehouse that will soon be a huge brewery. ("Why is there a canoe in their parking lot?" we ask.) After a sharp turn, we are suddenly in a back courtyard. (We wonder, "When did Leesburg get a Caribbean garden?") We slip in through another door and are heading up a stairway to a set of offices. Disoriented, we expect to run into Matt Damon and the Adjustment Bureau at any moment. Devine has a vision and plan for each of these buildings; and as we run through, he enthusiastically points out the meticulous details of each ("Look at these large pocket doors and this original fireplace!" he exclaims.)

Leesburg is a maze of preserved history—thanks to Devine's intervention. He has brought in diversity while preserving the integrity of the town. We end the tour at Devine's pride and joy which, according to him, is the sexiest building in Leesburg—the Tally Ho. Built in 1932 and originally operated as a motion picture and performing arts site, legend has it that Devine bought it for a dollar. He claims it was for a "cheap song." Now, it is a music venue the he co-owns with his son Jack, modeled after D.C.'s famous 9:30 Club. The Tally Ho Theatre is yet another example of Devine changing the landscape of Leesburg, while leaving the history intact. 🍸

Tally Ho mascot painted by
Devine's daughter, Ripley-Reece >

PRESERVING THROUGH THE ARTS

An interest in preservation runs in the Devine family. Jack Devine, Don's son, co-owns the Tally Ho Theatre, a live music venue in historic downtown Leesburg. The art deco building served as a movie theater for more than 80 years, but a decision was made to convert to live music when movie sales started dropping and newer multiplexes popped up. Jack had just graduated from college and was considering medical school when they began discussing the idea.

Jack had always had an interest in music, and even booked bands for his fraternity during college. "The idea of changing the Tally Ho around into a music venue got me excited," Jack says. He wanted to offer a place for his friends and others in Loudoun County to hear good music. Jack drew inspiration from his study abroad. "The music scene in Scotland was so diverse, you can see all these great bands up close. So I thought, 'Why couldn't that happen here?'" Father and son refurbished the inside and it can now hold as many as 750 people. The revamped venue brings a new energy to Leesburg, not just by preserving a historical building, but also by providing entertainment for multiple generations.

∧ Don and his son Jack inside the Tally Ho Theatre

Chicago-Style Topping Ideas

From Angel Miranda at Windy City Red Hots
Serves 1

INGREDIENTS:

Classic green relish

Yellow mustard

Sport peppers

Hot giardiniera peppers

Dill pickle spear

Diced tomatoes

Dash of celery salt

DIRECTIONS:

To make a true Chicago dog at home, add the following toppings to your favorite 100 percent beef hot dog or Polish sausage. It's like taking a trip to the Windy City while staying in the comfort of your own home!

It's a long list, but trust us—the flavor and fun you'll experience while eating it is well worth the extra time. If local to the Leesburg area, or when visiting, you can pick up jars of sport peppers and hot giardiniera peppers at Windy City Red Hots.

Curry Shrimp

From Herman Llewellyn at Blue Mountain Cafe
Serves 4

INGREDIENTS:

2 onions

2 scallions

1 hot pepper
  (ideally Scotch Bonnet)

4 cloves of garlic

1 bell pepper, red or orange

2 pounds of shrimp, peeled
  and deveined

2 tablespoons of Jamaican
  curry powder, divided

2 tablespoons of butter

½ teaspoon of salt

½ teaspoon of pepper

2 cups cooked rice

DIRECTIONS:

Chop the onion, scallion, pepper, garlic, and bell pepper. In a bowl, mix the shrimp with one tablespoon of curry powder.

Melt the butter in a large pan and add the other tablespoon of curry powder. Sauté for about one minute. Add the onion, scallion, pepper, garlic, tomato, sweet pepper, garlic, salt, and pepper to the pan. Sauté for about five minutes.

Add the shrimp and stir. Cover and simmer for about five minutes.

Serve with rice.

Coco Bread

From Herman Llewellyn at Blue Mountain Café
Serves 8

INGREDIENTS:

2 packages yeast

1 teaspoon sugar

¼ cup warm water

¾ cup warm coconut milk

1 ½ teaspoons salt

1 lightly beaten egg

3 cups flour

½ cup melted butter

Vegetable or coconut oil
   for greasing

DIRECTIONS:

Dissolve yeast and sugar in water. Stir in milk, salt, and egg. Add half of the flour and stir, continue to add flour until you have dough that can be turned out of the bowl.

Turn dough out on floured surface and knead for 10 minutes until smooth but firm. Oil a clean bowl and turn the dough in it until coated. Cover the bowl with a damp towel and let it rise for one hour.

Cut dough into half, and then cut into halves again until you have eight even pieces. Roll each piece into a 6-inch diameter circle. Brush with melted butter then fold in half. Brush with more butter and fold in half again. Set breads on an oiled baking sheet and let them rise until they double in size.

Preheat oven to 425°F and set a pan of hot water on the lowest oven rack. Place in the middle of upper rack and bake for about 12 to 15 minutes or until golden brown.

SHOE'S CUP AND CORK

Saving Soles

Responsibility is a heavy burden, especially when you have the responsibility of preserving the soul of Leesburg. When Fred and Karen Schaufeld decided to take over the ownership of the building that housed Shoe's Cup and Cork restaurant, they had a big decision to make – sell the building for a profit or try and keep the struggling coffee shop open.

17 N King St
Leesburg, VA 20176

shoescupandcork.com

Before it was converted into a coffee shop in 2009, the historic building had taken on many lives. It was a carriage repair shop, a post office, and then Arthur's Shoe Repair for 34 years before the 2009 transformation. There is still a generation of residents who credit Arthur with "saving their soles."

The Schaufelds feel it is important to uphold this town and its history to share with the next generation. "In Leesburg, we are fortunate to live among so much history; it's important to protect it and appreciate it." For this reason, Shoe's is proud to be part of the revitalization movement for downtown Leesburg.

The Schaufelds understood their obligation to Leesburg when they got the key to the building. "Shoe's has the old soul of Leesburg trapped in its walls," they say. While the coffee shop was not making money, they saw the importance of offering a place downtown for people to congregate. The unconventional look and feel of Shoe's is a breath of fresh air with its featured sloped wooden floors, antique brass shoe pedals which adorn the stools at the front windows, and boots hanging from the chandeliers. The clientele is truly a melting pot of souls—writers tapping along to Sinatra music, grandparents meeting preschoolers for lunch, and lawyers and clients discussing courtroom strategy for their trial across the street. "It's a quirky antidote to chain store life," explain the Schaufelds. "Leesburg is beautiful, historic, fun and it has character. We need a place that reflects that character and that is representative of Leesburg."

< Antique brass shoe pedals are leftover from when the space was Arthur's Shoe Repair

<< A chandelier made of old shoes hangs in the main dining room of Shoe's Cup and Cork

Shoe's is not only known for its past, but it is also known for being full of secrets. Behind the building and hidden from sight is a secret garden, accessible only through the type of narrow brick alleyway your mother always warned you to avoid. The alley opens up to a large outdoor patio decorated with twinkly lights and cabanas—and a full bocce ball court. With full menu service, live music, and heat lamps, it is a perfect location for a casual outdoor gathering with friends.

Upstairs is another well-kept secret—the Poker Room. Designed after an authentic speakeasy, it is only accessible through a secret sliding door and up a narrow brick stairwell. This private dining area transports guests back to the 1920s with its wood paneled walls, leather seats, era-period art and music. With so many alternatives, there is a place for every soul at Shoe's. 🎷

The secret passageway to the garden behind Shoe's Cup and Cork >

Bird in a Nest

From Shoe's Cup and Cork
Serves 1

INGREDIENTS:

1 teaspoon white wine vinegar

1 teaspoon salt

2 eggs

1 slice of multigrain bread

Kosher salt

Freshly cracked black pepper

DIRECTIONS:

Begin toasting the bread in toaster.

Fill a large pot with water. Add vinegar and salt and bring to a boil. Immediately turn off heat and cover the pot.

Crack the eggs, one at a time, into a small bowl and check for any shells.

Carefully place each egg, one at a time, into the water. Poach for four to five minutes. The yolks should be runny when done; do not over-cook.

While the eggs poach, cut a hole in the middle of the slice of toast and position in the middle of a serving plate. Carefully place the eggs in the hole and season with salt and pepper. Serve immediately.

Curried Cauliflower and Chickpeas

From Shoe's Cup and Cork
Serves 4 to 6 as a side

INGREDIENTS:

*Curried cauliflower
and chickpeas:*

Vegetable or canola oil,
   for frying

2 large eggs

Splash of milk or water

¼ cup all purpose flour

1 teaspoon kosher salt

½ teaspoon black pepper

2 cups fresh cauliflower florets

½ cup chickpeas

½ teaspoon curry powder

½ teaspoon cumin

½ teaspoon sea salt

¼ cup sliced pickled red
   peppers (such as Peppadew)

2 tablespoons lemon aioli

Lemon aioli:

½ cup mayonnaise

1 clove garlic, minced

¼ cup lemon juice

½ teaspoon lemon zest

1 teaspoon Dijon mustard

Kosher salt and freshly ground
   black pepper

DIRECTIONS:

In a large skillet or heavy-bottomed pot, add enough oil until it coats the sides up to to two inches. Heat over medium-high heat. The oil is ready when you drop a small bit of bread (or an extra chickpea) into it, and it immediately sizzles and bubbles over the food, frying it.

While the oil heats, beat the eggs in a large bowl until they are well scrambled and then add a splash of milk or water. In a separate large bowl, mix together the flour, kosher salt, and black pepper. Next, dredge the cauliflower by first adding it to the bowl with the egg wash (cover all florets) before transferring the cauliflower to the flour bowl and tossing the florets until they are well coated. Repeat the dredging process with the chickpeas. Prepare a large plate or baking sheet by lining it with paper towels and set to the side near the frying pan.

Fry the cauliflower and chickpeas for five to eight minutes until the cauliflower is golden and chickpeas are blistered. You may need to work in two batches depending upon the size of your frying pan. Remove cauliflower and chickpeas from the oil when done and let dry for one minute on the plate or baking sheet.

When slightly dry, remove the paper towels from the bottom of the plate and sprinkle the seasonings (curry powder through sea salt) on top of the vegetables. Toss to combine. Then, transfer to a plate or bowl for serving. Add pickled red peppers and drizzle on the lemon aioli.

STONE TOWER

Virginia is for Lovers

Kristi Huber has found her place in life; you can
see it in her eyes. She simply belongs overlooking
the vineyards at Stone Tower Winery on Hogback
Mountain, which she opened with her husband Mike
Huber in 2012. Since then, the two have created one
of the most beautiful vineyards and event venues in
Western Loudoun, and they did so because they simply
wanted to share the beauty of the land with others.

19925 Hogback Mountain Rd
Leesburg, VA 20175

stonetowerwinery.com

"When you look at the hills and views behind us, you just realize that it needs to be shared," Kristi explained one morning over tea. "And, that's really why we're here—we want to share this with people because it's incredible. When people bring their friends here from California, or really anywhere, they come and look and say, 'Wow! Virginia is beautiful.' And, it is. It really is."

Stone Tower's vista is in stark contrast to the Huber's first business venture together, Belfort Furniture, located 20 miles to the east, off of Route 28 in Sterling. This long established company, in the greater Northern Virginia region, has been the duo's project over the past 28 years. When Mike was young, his parents started a furniture business while stationed in Germany. Rumor has it that they got the idea to sell furniture after some army pals of Mike's dad commented on their nice dining room table over a friendly game of poker. Following in his parents' footsteps, Mike and Kristi founded Belfort Furniture, which has grown from a small 4,500 square foot warehouse space to an entire retail center comprised of multiple showrooms.

Mike and Kristi's family came to know and love Hogback Mountain, a peak along the southern edge of the Catoctin Mountain range. The elder Hubers had purchased a large swath of land that they used to raise cattle and horses. Over the years, frequent visits to this farm setting by Mike, Kristi and their three children prompted them to jump on the purchase of a neighboring parcel in the early 2000s, and they, too, soon found themselves owners of over 200 acres of property on Hogback Mountain.

"We really didn't know what we were going to do with it when we first bought it. We had just made a promise to ourselves that if the land ever went up for sale, then we would buy it. And then Mike had the idea to do wine because of the rolling hills," Kristi explains. That idea led to a shared vision of creating two new things: the first being a line of fine wines to be made using estate-grown grapes, and second, a space for others to enjoy and to use for various life events and pleasures.

∧ Stone Tower offers unique event spaces of all sizes

<< The rolling hills of Hogback Mountain

Once the vision was in place, they quickly moved full steam ahead. Kristi admits, "If Mike starts something, he knows that he'll do it well. He just has this belief in himself and in us. I believe in him, and, we just go do it."

Once the land was secured and the idea of a vineyard cast, professionals including two geologists and a viticulturist were brought in to help. They assessed soil conditions and worked to develop planting schedules. It was determined that many Vitis vinifera (classical) grape varietals would grow well on the land, particularly French varietals such as chardonnay, cabernet franc, merlot, and petit verdot. This led to an initial planting of 35 acres, an amount that has since almost doubled in the past two years. The Hubers found winemaker Tim Crowe, who had spent over two decades perfecting his craft in California, New Zealand, and Germany. Crowe used his expertise to establish a plan for making both estate wines and blends for Stone Tower's second label, Wild Boar Cellars. Additionally, daughter Lacey Huber joined the team, and was tasked with leading the tasting room experience and events. Lacey's passion for the business is shared by talented tasting room and events staff. Together, they create unforgettable experiences for every guest that enters the winery's doors.

< Lacey Huber pours a tasting at Stone Tower Winery

This classic farm truck makes for great engagement and wedding photos >>

A barn with sliding wooden doors and windows that open to the mountains was constructed to house a family-friendly tasting room. Nearby, a second facility, more industrial and spacious in nature with its cathedral-height ceilings, wide walkways and two rows of 20-feet tall oak and stainless tanks, was built to house additional tasting, event and winemaking areas including a new adults-only tasting room. Narrow, dimly lit hallways lead visitors from one room to the next, and give the impression of maneuvering through a cave. And, of course, the furnishings are lovely and modern, as would be expected.

Kristi and Lacey now work alongside each other to oversee Stone Tower's day-to-day operations, sales and events. One area that they especially enjoy are the weddings, something that Kristi was eager to start. It is not surprising that they have seen a lot of success given the popularity of winery weddings in Northern Virginia.

Lacey claims that her mom is the "hostess with the mostess" who really started the winery because she wanted to be able to host parties for the rest of her life. Kristi agrees, and says, "Not a wedding goes by where we don't cry. It's when the music starts and the bride begins to walk down the aisle. I'll look to Lacey and see we're both tearing up, and we just can't help it. Gosh, I love it so much. Oh, and the first dance—that always gets me!"

And with that, she turns back to the view before us—one of her own true loves. "It's so special. Every time, it is so special," she says, and we are left wondering whether she's referring to the weddings or the sight of the mountains before us. ❧

Clam Chowder

From Kristi Huber at Stone Tower Winery
Serves 8 as an appetizer, or 4 as a main course

INGREDIENTS:

1 ½ cups fresh chopped clams or
   4 (6 ½) ounce cans with juice

½ pound bacon,
   sliced into lardons

1 tablespoon unsalted butter

1 large diced onion

3 chopped celery stalks
   including greens

3 cloves minced garlic

2 tablespoons chopped
   fresh parsley

1 pound diced Russet Idaho
   potatoes (half-inch cubes)

4 tablespoons of
   all purpose flour

2 bay leaves

2 (10-ounce) bottles
   of clam juice

2 (12-ounce) cans of
   evaporated milk

1 cup heavy cream

¼ cup of chopped chives
   for topping

2 teaspoons Tabasco Sauce

Salt and pepper to taste

Stone Tower's Clam Chowder
pairs well with Stone Tower
Estate Chardonnay.

DIRECTIONS:

If using canned clams, drain their juice and reserve it to use with the bottled clam juice. Chop the clams into bite-sized pieces. If using fresh clams, clean and chop the clams and set to the side.

Heat a large, heavy-bottomed pot over medium-high heat. Add the bacon when hot and fry until color has deepened and the meat is slightly crisp. Remove when done and place slices on a plate lined with a paper towel to dry. Drain the bacon fat from the pan, leaving two to three teaspoons.

Reduce heat to medium and add one tablespoon of butter to the pot. When melted, add the chopped onions, celery, garlic and parsley and stir for three to four minutes. The onions should begin to look translucent.

Stir in the diced potatoes, flour, bay leaves, and both bottled and reserved clam juice and increase heat to high. Bring the liquid to a boil, then reduce the heat to medium-low and stir occasionally for 8 to 10 minutes. The sauce will thicken during this time and potatoes should soften.

In a separate small sauce pan, add the evaporated milk, heavy cream, and drained, chopped clams over medium-low heat for 5 to 7 minutes. Add the clam and cream mixture to the soup base when potatoes are soft. Simmer together for another 2 to 3 minutes so the flavors combine.

Add the Tabasco Sauce, then season with salt and pepper to taste. Stir to combine, then divide into bowls. Top with a sprinkle of chopped chives and bacon before serving, and enjoy!

Growing up in Seattle, we often visited my grandparents' beach house on Camano Island. We would fish, pick wild blackberries, pull in the crab pots, and my favorite was digging for clams. They were wonderful and plentiful! Here is a blend of my family's recipes. *– Kristi Huber*

Grilled Grape and Blue Cheese Pizza

From Kristi Huber at Stone Tower Winery
Serves 4

INGREDIENTS:

1 (16-ounce) package of store bought pizza dough, divided

3 tablespoons olive oil, divided

1 thinly sliced large Vidalia onion

1 cup ground cornmeal

1 ½ cups halved seedless red or green grapes

1 ½ cups crumbled blue cheese

1 tablespoon chopped fresh basil

Balsamic vinegar or glaze (store-bought is fine)

Salt and pepper to taste

Stone Tower's Grilled Grape and Blue Cheese Pizza pairs well with Stone Tower Estate Rosé and Wild Boar Malbec.

This is a great recipe that Dan, my brother-in-law, loves to make when cooking for large crowds at the winery. It's simple and so tasty. We use our own grapes if available! – *Kristi Huber*

DIRECTIONS:

Prepare and preheat the grill that you plan to use for cooking. This is especially important if using a charcoal grill and will ensure that the grill is ready by the time that you are ready to cook the pizzas.

About ten minutes before you begin to cook, pull the pizza dough out of the refrigerator and place into a bowl. Allow it to warm to room temperature and then divide the dough so that it's split into two halves.

In a large sauté pan, add one tablespoon of olive oil and heat over medium. Add onions and sauté for 8 to 12 minutes until golden brown and slightly caramelized.

While the onions cook, pour cornmeal onto a flat, nonporous surface (countertop or cutting board, for example) and spread the mounds of dough using a rolling pin into two pizza crusts roughly ½" to ¾" thick.

Turn grill to medium and brush the grill rack with 1 tablespoon olive oil. Brush the dough with ½ tablespoon olive oil and place it on the grill, oiled side down. Then brush the top of the dough using the remaining olive oil. Cover the grill and cook for about 90 seconds, until the bottom of the dough is golden brown. Remove the dough from the grill, cooked side facing up.

Add sautéed onions, grapes, blue cheese, and basil strips to the pizza. Drizzle the pizza with balsamic glaze and add salt and pepper to taste.

Place the pizza back on the grill until the cheese is partially melted—about three minutes. Transfer the pizza onto a cutting board, let cool for a minute, and slice. Enjoy!

LOVETTSVILLE
OLDE TOWN

PIZZA & SUBS
→
BEER

M.L. Shores Construction

CUSTOM HOMES & CARPENTRY
301-898-5073   540-822-5850

Bee Healthy Market
For the Love of Good Food

Pasture Raised Eggs   Organic Produce   Grass Fed Organic Dairy

Organic Meat and Poultry

Open Daily 9am - 8pm Closed Sunday

GROCERIES

LOVETTSVILLE

Lovettsville is a small town located on the northern tip of Virginia on the banks of the Potomac River. The town was originally settled by German immigrants in the 1730s, and is well known for its Oktoberfest and Christmas Market.

THE RESTAURANT AT PATOWMACK FARM

Patowmack Pioneer

Rebellious. Sage. Pioneering. Industrious. Kind. These words come to mind during the ninety minutes we spend with Beverly Morton Billand as she explains how she went from registered nurse to organic farmer to the owner of one of the most popular fine-dining restaurants in the region. We half expect to see her face next to the word "gumption" in *Merriam-Webster's Dictionary*.

42461 Lovettsville Rd
Lovettsville, VA 20180

patowmackfarm.com

The founder and owner of The Restaurant at Patowmack Farm did not set out to be a trailblazer in sustainable and organic agriculture, and she definitely did not plan on entering the fine-dining world. Rather, she set out with a very simple goal: to feed her family a healthy diet. "I knew that if I could grow my children's food and preserve and process it, that no matter what happened in my life, they would never go hungry," Morton Billand explains. "I thought that eating food grown without pesticides—I didn't know that it was called organic at the time—was just the normal way to eat, and so I wanted to share that with others."

The desire to grow food for her family was fostered in the 1960s, which Morton Billand explains was when she first learned of research about the effects of using chemicals in agriculture. As a nurse, she wanted to feed her children well, but was confused by nutrition reports because while they stated that eating fresh fruits and vegetables was healthy, they also showed that the chemicals used to grow them might have negative effects on the body.

She decided to do things her own way and grow her own food to feed her family. She began to look for farmland and eventually found a 40-acre, heavily wooded property in Northwestern Virginia that abuts the Potomac River. A realtor stumbled upon it, and while Morton Billand immediately felt drawn to it, she needed reassurance from her parents. After driving out to inspect it, her father cast his vote of approval and encouraged her to make the leap. "He said, 'Beverly, you must buy this property.' And so I did. He saw the vision for it," she reminisces as she looks wistfully toward the river and into another time.

Morton Billand began to farm in a way that encouraged the natural vitality of the land. She used natural fertilizers and crop cover rather than pesticides, herbicides, and chemicals. In addition, she also studied at the Rodale Institute in Pennsylvania, which many consider to be pioneering the organic movement.

∧ The restaurant is surrounded by glass on three sides and is situated right in the middle of Patowmack Farm

<< Patowmack Farm overlooks the Potomac River

After successfully growing various crops, Morton Billand decided to sell her surplus at the local farmer's market in an effort to bring in more income and not waste food. However, she quickly realized that she could not farm and work the market at the same time because the market pulled her away from plants she relied on for food and money. That led her to create a plan to bring shoppers directly to Patowmack Farm. She began to offer farm tours, which created an opportunity for soup lunches for those who toured the grounds, and eventually those evolved into farm dinners, where she served local wine.

One of the more humorous memories she has is of an official from Virginia's Alcoholic Beverage Commission (ABC) stopping by her home one day when she was by herself. She was running on a treadmill in the basement. "Here I was all alone, and I was not about to let some strange man into my house! Eventually, only after he tried to convince me for many minutes and showed me his ID badge, did I believe him. He told me what I was doing was illegal (selling wine at dinner), and that I needed to have a license." Raising her eyebrows wryly, she admits that she thought that she may need some sort of permission from the local government to serve alcohol, but as per usual, she took her chances and did it her way until told otherwise.

The farm dinners continued to grow in popularity, and, in 1998, she decided to go all-in and open a restaurant. *The Washington Post* ran a story about the restaurant shortly thereafter, and the write-up skyrocketed her into the world of food stardom. By 2000, she decided to hire a full-time chef to run the restaurant, and since then, several chefs have helped carry out her mission of providing high-quality, seasonal organic meals.

< Chef Tarver King cooks with the freshest ingredients right from the fields

Chickens enjoy their freedom to roam on the farm >>

> "There's nothing like clipping asparagus straight at the ground and then walking it 15 feet to a hot pan in the kitchen."

In 2013, Chef Tarver King took the reins and elevated the restaurant to a new level. King not only helps grow and harvest the ingredients on the property, but he has also created a variety of new prix fixe and à la carte dining options. He was nominated in 2015 for a James Beard Award, the same year that a *U.S.A. Today* Readers' Choice poll recognized the Restaurant at Patowmack Farm as one of the Best Fine Dining Restaurants in the South.

"There's nothing like clipping asparagus straight at the ground and then walking it 15 feet to a hot pan in the kitchen," King shares. "It is a privilege to cook this way, and it just tastes phenomenal!"

King and Morton Billand work with neighboring farms and producers to buy the ingredients that they don't grow themselves. "Every produce, herb, and plant that we use is grown or foraged for here," says King while pointing out beds of rosemary and basil right at the entrance to the restaurant. "We raise chickens and geese but only for their eggs. The only distributors I use are for meats, cheeses, and other dairy, and they're all local and organic, too, or CNG."

CNG, or Certified Naturally Grown, is Morton Billand's new standard for the farm. The certification was founded in New York in 2002 by husband-and-wife farmer team Ron and Kate Khosla. It is ideal for smaller farms that don't want to pay the hefty annual fees for the USDA's Certified Organic label, but still wish to grow and sell their wares according to strict standards.

Without a doubt, Morton Billand has succeeded in her early goal of providing food for her family and has surpassed it by opening her restaurant to feed others. She could retire if she wanted, but there are too many things to do on the farm and too many ideas in this pioneer's head to think about sitting back and simply enjoying the view of the Potomac. 🐓

Best Ever Fried Chicken

From Tarver King at the Restaurant at Patowmack Farm
Serves 4

INGREDIENTS:

2 large quartered chickens,
   do not de-bone

Grapeseed oil for frying

For the brine:

2 quarts water

1 cup kosher salt

½ cup sugar

1 cup thinly sliced garlic
   (6 to 8 cloves)

4 bay leaves

2 quarts buttermilk

For the flour dredge:

¼ cup ground black pepper

2 tablespoons pimenton de
   vera (or any ground chili
   pepper)

¼ cup herbes de provence

½ cup dried sage

6 cups cake flour

½ cup dried parsley

2 tablespoons onion powder

For the egg bath:

9 eggs

2 teaspoons baking powder

1 teaspoon baking soda

1 cup buttermilk

DIRECTIONS:

First make the brine. In a large pot, heat the water, salt, sugar, garlic, and bay leaves to a boil. Turn off once at a rolling boil and let sit until cool. Stir a few times to help dissolve the salt and sugar. When cooled, stir in the buttermilk.

Put the chicken into a snug container and pour the brine over it. Make sure that the chicken is submerged by weighing it down with a plate. Let the chicken brine in the refrigerator overnight.

The next day, mix all ingredients of the flour dredge (black pepper through onion powder). Place the dredge in a shallow dish big enough to fit the quartered pieces of chicken. Take the chicken out and rinse the brine off with cold water. Dry the chicken with a clean towel.

Mix the egg mixture together in a large bowl (it should be frothy). Toss the chicken in the egg and let sit for three to five minutes. Then, transfer the pieces to the flour dredge and bread the chicken. Coat heavily and thoroughly. Spread the chicken out on a tray, cover loosely with plastic wrap and return to the fridge for at least an hour. This will soften the flour and create sticky "dough" on the chicken.

Chef Tarver King swears by this recipe for the best ever fried chicken, even going so far to explain that having a really frothy egg bath "helps make a crazy good and crunchy texture" on the chicken's skin.

Fill two deep cast iron pans (ones that are large enough to hold all the chicken pieces) until they are both half-full with grapeseed oil. Heat to 340°F (you can use a candy thermometer or other heat-safe thermometer to do this). Additionally, heat the oven to 340°F. Have a separate large baking dish or cookie sheet lined with paper towels ready to rest the chicken on when it's cooked.

Add the chicken to the hot oil. Spread the chicken out in the pan as much as possible to keep from touching and slide the pans into the oven. Let the chicken fry slowly in the oven for 25 to 30 minutes, until the bottom half of the chicken is nicely browned.

Carefully take the hot pans out of the oven, and return to the burners on medium heat to finish frying. Turn the chicken pieces over and let brown for another 10 to 15 minutes on the other side so the chicken is thoroughly browned and cooked through.

Drain the chicken on the dish lined with paper towel, and let rest for a few minutes. Serve with your favorite hot sauce and cold beer.

This recipe is not as difficult as it looks, but does require a small time commitment split over two days—the first day is used to brine the chicken and the second to cook it. Having a couple of deep cast iron skillets or other heavy-bottomed pans on hand will ensure an even fry. – *Tarver King*

Butter Lettuce Salad with Buttermilk Dressing and Mussels

From Tarver King at the Restaurant at Patowmack Farm
Serves 4

INGREDIENTS:

For the salad:

3 large heads of butter lettuce

For the mussels:

2 cups dry white wine

6 cloves of crushed garlic

2 pounds of cleaned, large
  black mussels

½ cup olive oil

3 sliced shallots

3 to 4 sprigs of fresh dill

For the dressing:

2 cups sour cream

¼ cup buttermilk

¼ cup mussel cooking liquid

2 cloves minced garlic

¼ cup mayonnaise

2 tablespoons
  apple cider vinegar

1 tablespoon
  Worcestershire sauce

¼ cup grated Asiago cheese

½ tablespoon sugar

1 tablespoon salt

¼ tablespoon ground white
  pepper (sub in black if you
  don't have white available)

6 large leaves of
  minced fresh basil

6 to 8 springs of
  sliced fresh chives

3 to 4 sprigs of
  chopped fresh parsley

This spring salad is best if using lettuce and herbs fresh from the farmers' market or your own garden if you have a green thumb. – *Tarver King*

DIRECTIONS:

Prepare the salad: Pull the lettuce leaves from the core and wash in cold water. Use a salad spinner to dry the leaves (shake gently in a colander if you don't have a salad spinner), and then keep cold in a bowl in the fridge.

Prepare the mussels: In a large pot with a tight-fitting lid, slowly bring the wine to a simmer with garlic and shallots (do not boil). Let simmer for 20 to 30 minutes until the alcohol is cooked off and then add the olive oil. Add the mussels, toss them around to warm them, and cover with the lid. Let steam for 2 to 3 minutes.

Open the lid, and take out any mussels that have opened and set them on a plate to cool. Re-cover with the lid and steam for one more minute. Take out any that have opened and let cool on a plate. Keep the process going until they are all cooked. If there are any that do not open, throw them away. Let the mussels cool enough to be handled.

While the mussels cool, slowly reduce the wine and cooking juices in the pot over medium-low or medium heat until about half of the liquid remains. Transfer the liquid to a smaller container that has a lid. Clean the mussels of their shells and add to the cooking juices. Cover, and keep cool in the fridge.

Prepare the dressing: Blend the first 11 ingredients, from sour cream to white pepper, in a blender until smooth. Stir in the herbs and keep cool.

Compile the salad: In a large bowl, dress the leaves with the dressing, and add the mussels. Season with kosher or sea salt and divide between four plates. Add fresh sprigs of parsley and cracked pepper.

MARKET TABLE BISTRO

An Education in Food

13 E Broad Way
Lovettsville, VA 20180

markettablebistro.com

A wave of sweetly scented smoke billows out from the bottom of the glass as it is lifted from the wood board, almost as if it were an upside-down tornado. The smell of the aptly named dessert, "Sittin' By the Campfire," is confusing. While our noses register the scent of burning wood, our eyes and ears remind us that we are actually sitting inside an old home turned restaurant, tucked away in one of the northernmost points of Virginia. The dessert, which uses a small gun to inject smoke into the marshmallow, graham cracker, and dark chocolate dish, is just one of the many surprises and creative twists on the dinner menu at Market Table Bistro.

"We're doing all sorts of fun things here," Executive Chef Jason Lage states matter-of-factly, before circling back to the kitchen where a plastic tub of freshly harvested ramps was just dropped off by a local farmer.

You can hear the excitement about food in Lage's voice as he talks about what you can do with simple, fresh ingredients. He and business partner/General Manager Rebecca Dudley are paving a path in Western Loudoun, hoping to educate consumers about the simplicity of food, the importance of seasonality, and hospitality.

Lage and Dudley met while working at Lansdowne Resort in Leesburg, which typically gets more visitors in a day than Lovettsville has residents. After working for years in some of Washington, D.C.'s most prominent restaurants, as well as in restaurant settings abroad, they both yearned for a calmer environment and one that featured menu selections using the ingredients they love. Lovettsville provided the perfect setting for their first restaurant foray, given its low-key rural atmosphere, proximity to farms, and the year-round production of produce.

Chef Jason Lage
prepares a rabbit dish >

<< The comfortable dining room
is made to feel like you are eating
in the chef's house

"I always tell the staff that I want people to feel like they're in my house when they come into the restaurant," Lage explains. Luckily, the restaurant is housed in a 19th century home that still has large wooden beams and original wood floors in some areas. The surprisingly small kitchen is where dishes come alive.

Perhaps the biggest logistical challenge that the duo faces on an almost daily basis is in gathering ingredients. They source the majority of their foods from local suppliers throughout the region. There are limitations to ordering based not only on the season, but also on what the farmers are successful in growing.

"It would be so much easier for me to call up Coastal Sunbelt and order six cases of tomatoes if I wanted them," Lage explains. "But we don't want to do that." Rather, they buy from local farmers even though it means greater flexibility is required.

Dudley, who handles much of the procurement, finds that farms face money and priority challenges. "The smaller farms can't afford to have someone answering phones for orders, or the people who take the orders are out in the fields most of the day, and so you really have to work hard to get food from them," she says. "Logistically, it is much harder to buy this way."

Conversely, the seasonal items they do receive are a constant source of creativity for Lage and his team. The menus are updated regularly, sometimes daily, with the newest creations and list of suppliers. The chef likes to try new things, including molecular gastronomy as demonstrated in dishes like "Sittin' By the Campfire." He also knows not to tamper with ingredients too much.

"I think you lose the soul of food when you manipulate it too much," Lage says. "It's much better, but often harder, to keep things simple on a plate," he muses.

Educating customers about food, where it comes from, and when it's available is the passion that fuels the fire that Lage and Dudley continue to build together. The pair followed up the bistro with Market Burger in Purcellville in 2012. Market Burger offerings include locally raised beef, turkey, and veggie burgers, hand-cut fries and hand-dipped milkshakes made with locally produced ice cream.

< Lage's ultimate sensory dessert is Sittin' by the Campfire

A Mexican restaurant and tequila bar in Leesburg, slated for 2016, will be the third restaurant in their portfolio, and has been inspired by their travels to Mexico City, Oaxaca, Veracruz, and Puebla, Mexico. Though one may not realize it, Virginia has an ideal climate and soil for growing many ingredients that are common in Mexican dishes such as squash, peppers, garlic, and onions.

Lage and Dudley were able to showcase such ingredients earlier in 2015 after being invited to speak to a group of elementary school students about the farm-to-table movement in Western Loudoun. Lage brought ingredients and made a batch of salsa in front of the students to show them what tomatoes off the vine can become with just a little manipulation and seasoning.

"We want to continue to educate, especially young people, about how important it is to know where your food comes from. We want to support local farmers and make people happy. And just make good food! That's where we see ourselves growing and evolving in the future," Lage says with gusto.

Lage invited us for another visit to forage for mushrooms with him and a friend, someone the chef says is one of the best mushroom scavengers he's ever met. It's apparent that Chef Lage loves being hands-on in all aspects of his business initiatives.

A perfect spring meal of rabbit with carrots and celery root ∨

Butternut Squash Bisque

From Jason Lage at Market Table Bistro
Serves 8

INGREDIENTS:

¼ cup canola oil

1 large butternut squash
(approximately 1 to 2 pounds)
peeled, halved, seeded and
diced into 1 ½" pieces

1 small Spanish or red onion
diced in ½" pieces

3 Granny Smith apples
peeled, cored, diced
into large 2" pieces

1 teaspoon ground cinnamon

¼ cup light brown sugar

4 cups (1 quart) heavy cream

Kosher salt, to taste

Water as needed

Diced chives, optional

DIRECTIONS:

In a large, heavy-bottomed saucepot, heat the canola oil over medium-high heat and add the butternut squash. Sauté for five to six minutes making sure not to brown the squash. Add the onions and cook for an additional three to four minutes. Stir in the apples and cook for an additional two to three minutes.

Add the cinnamon and brown sugar and cook for three minutes; stir the mixture often during this time. Pour in the heavy cream and cook for 25 to 30 minutes at a medium simmer or until the squash is fork tender.

Carefully transfer the soup to a blender or food processor (you may need to work in batches) and process until it reaches the desired consistency. You may need to thin the mixture with a little water.

When blended, season with salt to taste and top with chives, if desired, before serving. You can keep any leftovers in the refrigerator for 7 to 10 days.

HILLSBORO

Hillsboro is the smallest, unincorporated town in Virginia. Named for being situated between large hills, it was settled more than 200 years ago and is well known for its beautiful stone buildings including the historic Old Stone School.

OLD 690 BREWING COMPANY

Change is Brewing in Hillsboro

Bright lines of green vines wind their way up vertically hung wires behind the main building of the Old 690 Brewing Company. It's only the second year that co-owners and friends Darren Gryniuk and Mark Powell have tried their hand at growing hops, but if you were to look at the thriving vines, you'd think that they had been doing it for much longer. But that's not how this duo operates; experimentation and action are more their style.

15670 Ashbury Church Rd
Purcellville, VA 20132

old690.com

Gryniuk and Powell have been friends and neighbors for more than a decade, and they spent about that much time coaching against one another in the Upper Loudoun Youth Football League while their sons were growing up. While they both loved to win and compete for bragging rights, they also enjoyed the bonding that often came over cold drinks after games ended. Powell was fondly referred to as the "King of Bud Light."

"We had a lot of bad beer while coaching," Gryniuk joked one afternoon. After enough bad beer, they reached a sipping point and decided they would be better off brewing their own.

<< Old 690 growlers line the wall

Darren Gryniuk behind
the bar at Old 690 v

Gryniuk knew that craft beer had been trending, so much so that it had begun to outpace the production and consumption of mass-produced brands in the early 2000s. This data, plus anecdotal feedback indicating that a local market of consumers would support a new brewery in Western Loudoun, led Gryniuk in 2013 to convince Powell that they should open a farm brewery and make their own craft beer. Powell and his wife, Ronda, owned 10 acres of pastoral land that would make the perfect site for a quaint, local brewery. There was also ample space to grow hops and other ingredients, like raspberries and herbs, which they could use to flavor the beers. Lastly, and most importantly, new state legislation that would establish a license for farm breweries to operate and sell beer in Virginia was making its rounds through the General Assembly. With the stars aligning, the duo began to build their brewery while counting on the passing legislation.

Gryniuk admitted that he wasn't afraid of failing at opening the business, even though neither he nor Powell considered themselves farmers or brewers. "I'd rather try and fail at this versus not try it at all," Gryniuk says. "It makes for a better life story to try." They're both entrepreneurs at heart and have dabbled in other self-made businesses before, so they thought of the brewery as just another new venture.

One thing they quickly realized was that they did not have the skills or experience to brew the beer they wished to sell, so they brought in a local expert to help. "Originally, we both thought that we could brew the beer ourselves. And then we kept reading and learning about it, and started to look at each other and say, 'Maybe we can't do that, actually,'" Gryniuk laughs. "So, we found Bob." Bob Lundberg, lovingly known as "Bob the Brewer," joined the team in December 2013 and began to refine various beer styles he'd been tinkering with at home for more than a decade.

In February 2014, the Virginia Senate created a specific license for farmers to brew beer and grow hops, and maintain a residence on the same property. This was exactly what Gryniuk and Powell needed to get their business off the ground. Old 690 Brewing Company opened in August, just one month after the legislation was signed into law by Virginia Governor Terry McAuliffe.

Gryniuk and his wife began a grassroots marketing and social media promotion to spread the word about the brewery's opening. A number of their beers, all with witty names inspired by neighbors who helped (or hindered) the brewery's formation, quickly became fast favorites with patrons, specifically the Bitter Neighbor IPA and the Happy Neighbor Belgian Tripel.

∧ Bumper art adorns the walls

< Ingredients for craft brews

For as much as Powell and Gryniuk had aligned themselves to the timing of the farm brewery law passing, they found they could not make Loudoun County leaders adopt the new regulations any faster than they were willing to do so. Just four months after opening, Old 690 Brewing Company was shut down for a three-week period until the county recognized the new law and granted them the zoning permit necessary to operate their farm brewery.

As frustrating as that was, Gryniuk saw some benefits from the brief shut down. For one, their patron base seemed to grow larger and stronger during the time that they weren't allowed to be open. Secondly, Old 690 became a guinea pig of sorts for other budding farm breweries in the county. Gryniuk and Powell hoped their experience would lead the way and, in fact, more than five other farm breweries have opened since Old 690 blazed the trail.

Today, Gryniuk, Powell and Lundberg all take turns working behind the bar at Old 690 on weekends. Day jobs still keep them busy during the workweek. Their families pitch in as well. Gryniuk and Powell each have a shared goal to one day work full-time at the brewery—a step that would include opening another facility. For now, they are enjoying seeing their business advance from "Can we do this?" to "How can we do it better and do it more?" And, of course, they've also enjoyed having better beer to drink after football games. 🍺

The rotating craft beer menu >

Bacon Cheddar Chive Muffins

From Joy's Dream Bakery
Makes 8 large muffins

INGREDIENTS:

2 cups all purpose flour

2 teaspoons baking powder

½ teaspoon salt

1 tablespoon sugar

1 ½ cups cooked, crumbled bacon (about 6 strips)

¼ cup fresh, finely chopped chives

2 cups shredded cheddar cheese, divided

2 eggs

1 stick melted butter, cooled

1 cup milk

½ cup sour cream

DIRECTIONS:

Preheat oven to 350°F. Line muffin tins with paper liners or spray with nonstick baking spray, then set aside.

Fry the bacon strips over medium-high heat in a cast iron or heavy bottomed skillet. When darkened, but not too crisp, remove to a plate lined with a paper towel to drain. When cooled slightly, crumble the strips and set aside.

Sift together flour, baking powder, salt, and sugar in a medium bowl. Stir bacon, chives, and one cup of cheddar cheese into flour mixture to coat. In a separate large bowl, combine the eggs, cooled melted butter, milk, and sour cream. Add flour mixture to wet ingredients and combine until mixture is wet. Do not over-mix, as this will create a tough muffin.

Fill muffin tins ¾ of the way up and top with the remaining cup of shredded cheddar cheese. Bake for 20 to 25 minutes, until the tops are lightly golden and a toothpick inserted into the center comes out mostly clean. Remove from oven and rest on cooling rack for 5 to 10 minutes before serving. Enjoy!

This recipe is another favorite from **Joy's Dream Bakery**, located in Purcellville. The savory cheddar and bacon flavors pair particularly well with the hoppy notes in Bitter Neighbor IPA, which you could pick up in a growler from Old 690.

BLUEMONT

Bluemont is a small village located on the eastern side of the Blue Ridge Mountains at the very edge of Loudoun County. Bordered by the Appalachian Trail and located high up in the mountains, the hamlet is an excellent destination for those who want to capture a great view of the region's peaks and valleys.

DIRT FARM BREWING

Farming and Beer: A Perfect Match

Up a steep drive to the top of the Blue Ridge Mountains sits Dirt Farm Brewing. A former weekend retreat home, the site makes a perfect tasting room for a laid back farm brewery. Couples and families sit around with pretzel bites and boiled peanuts, tasting flights of craft beer. Kids hide behind large trees and jump off boulders while adults enjoy the sweeping views overlooking all of Loudoun County.

18701 Foggy Bottom Rd
Bluemont, VA 20135

dirtfarmbrewing.com

∧ Janell Zurschmeide
behind the bar at
Dirt Farm Brewery

Dirt Farm Brewing is a recent addition to the Zurschmeide family's agricultural enterprise in Bluemont. The family has been in the farming business for over 35 years and employ a number of family members in various positions from kettle corn popper to vineyard owner. With more than 300 acres at the foothills of the Blue Ridge Mountains, the family has created an agritourism destination perfectly situated on the outskirts of the D.C. metro area with sweeping mountain views of the rural landscape. At the center of their operations is Great Country Farms, a working farm where families are invited to enjoy a number of activities such as U-pick fields, hay rides and seasonal activities. Their successful Community Supported Agriculture (CSA) program delivers more than 1,200 boxes of fresh produce around Northern Virginia each year.

"Farmers are uniquely positioned to bring the flavors of fruits and vegetables farmed from the Earth."

In 2007, the Zurschmeides established Bluemont Vineyard, a small boutique winery located across the road and up a steep hill from Great Country Farms. After many years of continued success of the winery, they decided to further expand their business and established a farm brewery along with a tasting room to serve their craft beer. The timing of their farm brewery worked well in that the state and local regulations, the same ones that impacted Old 690 Brewery for a period of time, were more established and observed in the county, which allowed for a smooth transition.

While farm breweries may be a new business in Loudoun County, it is certainly not a new concept. According to the Zurschmeide family, farms are the most obvious place to brew craft beer considering the access to resources. "Farmers are uniquely positioned to bring the flavors of fruits and vegetables farmed from the Earth," explain Janell and Kate Zurschmeide, sisters-in-law who co-own the brewery with their husbands, brothers Mark and Bruce. "The quality of the product starts in the ground."

Craft brewing has become a passion of Bruce and Janell. "There are so many ways to flavor and experiment in the craft beer environment; it provides a unique outlet for Bruce's naturally creative side," says Janell. Thanks to the family farm, they are able to experiment with all types of flavors—tart cherries, pumpkins, peaches and even sweet potatoes. At Dirt Farm Brewing, the Zurschmeides handcraft in small batches to allow for guest feedback before deciding which formulas to keep. They credit the strong professional community of craft breweries in the state of Virginia for helping them refine their techniques.

The Zurschmeides are excited by the role that farming will continue to play in the beer industry. Janell believes that "the resurgence of craft beverages is a huge catalyst to bring younger generations back to the farm. We see it as a key way to expand and provide our next generation the opportunity to keep farming. More farms are needed to meet the growing demand for raw materials, and sourcing as locally as possible is a key to the process. We recognize and embrace the opportunity to farm brew. We are driven by the endless possibilities of what craft beer can and will become."

Dirt Farm Boiled Peanuts

From Dirt Farm Brewery

INGREDIENTS:

2–3 pounds raw peanuts
  in the shell

Boiling water

Kosher salt

DIRECTIONS:

Rinse and drain raw peanuts.

Bring a large pot of water to a boil. While water heats, rinse and drain peanuts. Add peanuts to the pot and boil six to eight hours. Add salt to taste.

We fell in love with this southern tradition while touring the craft beer scene of North Carolina in 2013. Boiled peanuts pair nicely with beer. – *Janell Zurschmeide*

Open-Faced Peach Cobbler

From Great Country Farms
Serves 6

INGREDIENTS:

1 ready-made (store-bought) pie crust

6 peaches

2 tablespoons plus 2 teaspoons unsalted butter

2 teaspoons cinnamon

2 tablespoons sugar

DIRECTIONS:

Preheat oven to 350°F. Grease a medium-sized baking sheet with butter or nonstick baking spray.

On a non-porous surface, such as a counter or a wood cutting board, roll out the pie crust so that it is roughly the same size as the baking sheet. Transfer the crust onto the greased baking sheet and brush with 2 teaspoons melted butter.

Peel, pit, and slice peaches in half. Place each peach half on top of the dough, cut side up (space evenly across the dough). Place a pat of butter on each peach slice. Sprinkle the peach halves and crust with cinnamon and sugar. Bake for 15 to 20 minutes, until crust is golden and peaches have caramelized on top. Slice into 6 even pieces and serve.

This recipe is from Grandma Zurschmeide and has been a staple of summertime family dinner on the mountain. Farmer Bob Zurschmeide likes to joke that he put himself through college with money coated in peach fuzz. Harvesting peaches at Great Country Farms has become a family tradition and is a true way to bring the family together. Try adding blackberries for additional color and flavor. – *Janell Zurschmeide*

LINCOLN

Lincoln is an unincorporated village tucked away on gravel roads in the Goose Creek Historic District, located to the south of Purcellville. Established by Quakers in the 1740s, Lincoln is steeped in proud abolitionist history. Along its winding roads you will find many historic farmsteads as well as the Goose Creek Friends Meeting House, Goose Creek Historic District, an ancient Quaker cemetery, and Oakdale School, the oldest one-room brick school house in Loudoun County.

OAKLAND GREEN FARM

The Keeper of Stories

Sara Brown is a natural storyteller. She has a rich voice that carries a story like a melody, the chorus line usually her resonating laugh. Brown's ability to see her life through the narrative lens probably helps her survive the challenges of living on a 200-acre cattle farm that has been in her family for ten generations.

19192 Oakland Green Rd
Leesburg, VA 20175

oaklandgreen.com

^ Oakland Green sits on 200 acres of farm land in the heart of the Goose Creek Historic District

Guests at the farm can see their original land grant signed by Lord Fairfax in 1741 >>

"Nine out of ten days are good," she says, "but then that one day can be really awful. Somebody calls you at 6:30 in the morning asking if those are your 20 cows in the middle of the road because a tree fell on your fence and somebody decided to take a walk." She laughs at the memory—what started out as a tough morning is now just another story to add to her collection.

Brown and her husband, Scott Maison, own Oakland Green, a cattle farm in the heart of the Goose Creek Historic District. The district is a collection of land and small farms passed down from Virginia's largest concentration of Quaker settlers. Visiting the farm is more than a history lesson—it is visiting the living story of Virginia. The farm, which survived the Civil War, dates back to Virginia land grants and is said to have had the first bathroom in Loudoun County. Through careful preservation of family letters and artifacts, this farm maintains an incredibly personalized record of US history dating back to the 1700s. While Brown may be raising cattle and operating a bed and breakfast on property, her most prized role is unofficial docent of Virginia's history. She has preserved ten generations worth of family and local history, all while modernizing and maintaining the family farm.

Sitting on the wide front porch in the afternoon breeze, we look over a portrait-worthy landscape that is a testament to untouched natural beauty of more than 200 acres of farmland, generations of cultivated gardens, and trees that have been allowed to mature for more than a century.

Brown's story starts seven generations back with her grandfather, Richard Brown, one of the original Quaker settlers in the Goose Creek area. As a Quaker, Richard did not use slave labor for his farm. Instead, he and his wife had a number of children, and he relied upon his large family. Brown's grandfather originally built a log cabin on the property. Subsequent generations added a stone house, and then a brick house. The three houses were connected and now make up the homestead for Brown, her husband and their two children. The original log cabin was fully restored and now serves as a bed and breakfast where, thanks to a collection of family antiques, guests feel transported back to the 1700s, even though more modern conveniences are cleverly incorporated and tucked away. Now guests can enjoy a bag of microwaved popcorn as they look over the farm's original land grant signed by Lord Fairfax in 1741.

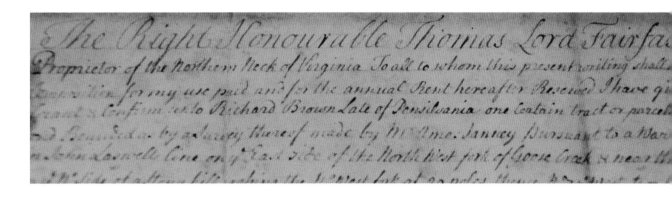

In the barn we stop to see the chickens and admire the pre-Civil War construction, one of the few barns to survive the notorious Loudoun County Burning Raid that destroyed most of the area's farmland. According to family legend, the Browns were standing on the edge of their property watching the surrounding farms burn when a hawk started to swoop at their chickens. They shot the hawk just as the Union militia was approaching their property, and when the soldiers heard gunfire, they turned around and left the property alone, which is the only reason it is still standing today.

When we ask if she ever wanted to leave Lincoln, Brown says she had no hesitations returning after college. "It's where I'm meant to be," she explains, adding that her criteria for any suitors meant they had to be accepting of her responsibilities on the farm. When she met her husband, who grew up on the New Jersey shore, she said he knew what he was getting into.

Before Brown married, her family put 186 acres into a conservation easement and kept 14 acres to which Sara added the cattle component. She had been raising cattle since her days in 4-H and felt this would be a way for her to bring in additional income and make an impact on her community. "I had feelings about the food system," Sara explains. She is very interested in the link between poverty and nutrition. "There is a systemic problem in our food system in the difference between what food really costs to make and what you buy it for," she says. Brown feels that if we continue to subsidize food that is actually expensive to make, then people on public assistance will continue to be forced to make unhealthy food choices due to cost.

Sara Brown continues to carry on family tradition, but when we ask if she will one day encourage her own children to take over the farm, she merely shrugs, "They have some big shoes to fill." For now, the children play freely in their yard and listen to their mother's stories. Who knows if these stories will take root, and one day they too will be their keepers? 🐾

< At Oakland Green, everyone
has a job to do, including Banjo

Perfect Beef Roast

From Sara Brown
Serves 6

INGREDIENTS:

1 ½ pounds eye round
   or sirloin tip roast

Kitchen string

2 tablespoons vegetable oil

Salt

Pepper

DIRECTIONS:

Preheat oven to 225°F.

Bring roast to room temperature. Wrap kitchen string around the roast and tie in a knot to keep it bundled. Season with plenty of salt, pepper, and any other herbs or spices you like.

Heat oil in a heavy skillet, preferably cast iron. Brown the roast on both sides and then remove to a plate. Place a meat rack in the skillet and return the roast to the rack, so that it's elevated from the bottom of the hot pan. Poke a meat thermometer into the thickest part of the meat.

Place the skillet in the oven and roast until the thermometer reaches 120°F; the beef will be rare at this point and will take roughly 75 to 90 minutes. Turn the oven off and let the roast stay inside until the meat's internal temperature reaches 130°F to 140°F, which is medium-rare to medium. This will take about 30 minutes for medium-rare or up to to 50 minutes for medium.

Remove skillet from oven and let meat rest for at least 10 minutes before slicing into medallions.

The key to a perfect roast is good equipment. My trick is a meat thermometer that has a cord to the outside of the oven. Having a good skillet with a rack is also important. – *Sara Brown*

French Toast

From Sara Brown
Serves 4

INGREDIENTS:

1 loaf of Italian bread,
    cut into 1-inch slices

1 ½ cups milk

6 eggs

½ cup Bisquick baking mix

2 tablespoons sugar

1 teaspoon cinnamon

½ teaspoon nutmeg

Vegetable oil for frying

DIRECTIONS:

Place bread slices that have been sitting out all night into a jelly roll pan or rectangular baking dish. Place milk, eggs, Bisquick, sugar, cinnamon, and nutmeg in the blender and mix until well blended. Pour over the bread. Let sit for an hour so that both sides soak up the custard.

Pour one inch of vegetable oil in a large, deep skillet with a lid. Heat oil to 275–285°F. Carefully add a bread slice to the oil. It should float freely in the oil and sizzle when added. If it does not sizzle, increase the heat and wait another minute or two for it to get hotter, then add a slice again. Working a few pieces at a time, cover the skillet and cook for three to five minutes. Uncover and flip the toast. Put lid back on for another two minutes.

When both sides are golden brown, remove from oil and drain on a cooling rack set over a cookie sheet. If needed, keep warm in 200°F oven. The toast may deflate slightly while you wait to serve, but it will still be light and airy.

Serve the French toast with some savory sausage, such as sage. Get real maple syrup—look at the ingredients to make sure you're getting syrup from a maple tree, not brown corn syrup. Some lumberjack ought to be on the bottle. It makes a huge difference. And serve with fruit because you cannot just serve sausage and deep fried bread. Serve fruit, too. – *Sara Brown*

The key to this French toast is prepping the night before. Start with one of those big fluffy Italian loaves from the bakery section at the grocery store. The night before, you need to slice it kind of thick—maybe an inch thick. I slice on the bias most of the time, but depending on the loaf it sometimes makes the pieces too big to fit nicely in my skillet. After you slice, set the pieces on a cooling rack that's placed on top of a cookie sheet so that air can flow to both sides. Leave out overnight in an ajar oven, only if you have a dog like mine who will eat everything you leave on the counter. Then use in the morning to make this recipe. — *Sara Brown*

WEGMEYER FARMS

Farmers for the People

Tyler and Harriet Wegmeyer are advocates for bringing farming back to the people. They both grew up on dairy farms and remember life on the farm as being hard but extremely rewarding. "The work ethic you learn on a family farm can take you through anything in life," Harriet says. "We want our kids to have the benefit of that lifestyle. Growing up on a farm, we know they will be able to handle anything that comes their way."

38299 Hughesville Rd
Hamilton, VA 20158

wegmeyerfarms.com

When the Wegmeyers first stepped foot on the 25-acre farm for sale in Lincoln, they knew it was exactly what they wanted. Harriet fell in love with the old farmhouse. Even though it was run-down, she saw its unique structure that just needed some love and care to make it work. Tyler had his heart set on the land. He saw the water source, rolling hills, and the landscape and knew it would make for a great farm.

They both had experience with pumpkins, so they started with a small crop to sell at local farmers' markets. They never had plans to open their home farm to the public, but customers kept asking to pick their own pumpkins and so they decided to give it a try. "It was very rewarding to see people happy. People who came to the farm knew us from the farmer's market; it all worked," Harriet says. "You start something and you don't know where your path is going to lead, and we are happy with where it has led us." They even turned their stone barn into a farm store.

Since the Wegmeyers' path was leading them to a U-pick farm model, they decided they needed to add another crop for a second season. When Tyler was in college at Michigan State, he put together a plan for a U-pick strawberry farm in Michigan. "He was so happy to pull out his old college plan and do it in Virginia," recalls Harriet. "We had no idea if it was going to be successful. We really had to learn and teach ourselves."

The couple enjoyed inviting the public to their farm so much that they expanded to other Virginia locations to provide different agricultural experiences. They opened a destination pumpkin farm in Berryville where they grow a U-pick field, provide a corn maze, organize charity races, and serve as the site for science-based field trips for regional schools. They aim to inspire the next generation of farmers, encourage people to enjoy the natural landscape, and appreciate the agricultural lifestyle.

<< Tyler Wegmeyer and his team wait for field trip students in the strawberry fields

Wegmeyers sells a variety of pumpkins in their old stone farm store v

Another passionate project of the Wegmeyer duo is celebrating local history through agriculture. While attending a local lecture, Harriet was struck by an idea to use farming to support Oatlands Plantation, built in the 1800s and now a National Historic Site in Leesburg. During the lecture, a local diary entry from 1861 mentioned the first strawberry of the season at Oatlands Plantation, and Harriet knew that would be a great way to bring history and farming to the people. "Oatlands is a gem; it is a beautiful piece of property and more people should know about it, so I thought this would be a great opportunity," says Harriet. The plantation used to grow strawberries in its greenhouse, known as the second oldest continuously cultivating greenhouse in the United States. The Oatlands families even hosted strawberry festivals to raise money for charities. By bringing strawberries back to the plantation, the Wegmeyers are tying Oatlands' history to modern day. The Wegmeyers and Oatlands have even created a field trip so students have a chance to learn about history and agriculture, all while interacting with growers dressed in period era costumes.

In addition to preserving history, the Wegmeyers hope to help with conservation by leasing U-pick acres in Gilbert's Corner, an area of approximately 400 acres in Loudoun County that is being preserved through the Northern Virginia Parks Authority and the Piedmont Environmental Council. The land was the site of a deadly 24-hour conflict between Union and Confederate battalions that killed or wounded more than 100 soldiers and caused the Union troops to retreat.

This historical landsite is also what some would consider to be a crossroads between suburban and rural Loudoun, making it a critical area for conservation. "There are so many families close to there who don't have access to agriculture in their backyard, but they can come out to Gilbert's Corner and experience agriculture first hand by picking their own produce. It's a great way for families to understand the rich land in our area and how things are grown," says Harriet Wegmeyer.

Picking buckets full of
strawberries in the U-pick fields v

Kristin's Strawberry Hand Pies

From Kristin O'Rourke and sold at Wegmeyer Farms
Serves 10

INGREDIENTS:

2 ¼ cups all purpose flour

2 teaspoons sugar

1 teaspoon salt

1 cup cold, unsalted butter
 cut into small pieces

1 large egg

2 tablespoons cold milk

1 ¾ cups hulled and quartered
 fresh strawberries

2 tablespoons sugar

2 teaspoons cornstarch

1 teaspoon fresh lemon juice

1 large beaten egg
 for sealing dough

Coarse white sugar for
 sprinkling

DIRECTIONS:

Using a food processor, pulse flour, sugar, and salt several times to combine. Add butter and pulse until pea size pieces form. Combine egg and milk in a small bowl, and add to food processor in a slow, steady stream while pulsing until dough is crumbly and holds together when pressed between fingers. Add an additional tablespoon of milk if needed. Do not over mix. Form dough into two discs, wrap tightly in plastic and refrigerate for at least one hour.

In a saucepan over medium heat, combine strawberries, sugar, cornstarch, and lemon juice. Cook for approximately five minutes, until the filling starts to thicken. Pour into a bowl to cool.

Preheat oven to 350°F and lightly grease a baking sheet or line with parchment paper. Prepare a work surface with flour and place one piece of dough in the center. Roll into a 6" x 20" rectangle and cut out five 6" x 4" rectangles. Repeat with the remaining dough. Place a heaping tablespoon of strawberry filling in the center of each rectangle, and then brush the egg wash along the edges. Fold each rectangle in half and press the edges with a fork to seal. Using a sharp knife, cut vents in the top of the pies. Brush the pies with the egg wash and sprinkle with sugar. Place pies on the baking sheet and bake for approximately 28 to 32 minutes, until the crust is golden brown. Remove from oven and place pies on a wire rack to cool. Enjoy warm or cool.

Kristin is a phenomenal baker. She volunteers to make the baked goods for newcomers who move into Lincoln Village. Her treats were always so good, we asked her to make a strawberry treat we could sell at the farm, and she made these. – *Harriet Wegmeyer*

LUCKETTS

Lucketts is a small village bordering the Potomac River that makes a perfect overnight getaway for a group of friends or family. Roads leading to the village are lined with charming antique stores and farm stands.

FAITH LIKE A
MUSTARD SEED FARM

The Philosophy of Farming

There is an island in Western Loudoun. It is the color of swirling sand and surrounded by philosophers. It sits in the middle of a gourmet kitchen in a historic farmhouse off a side road in Lucketts called Faith Like a Mustard Seed Farm.

42906 Lucketts Rd
Leesburg, VA 20176

faithlikeamustardseedfarm.com

The island's owner is Patricia Glaeser, a farmer, classically trained chef, and one of those thoughtful souls to whom people are magnetically attracted. She is smart and passionate and loves to philosophize on everything from heritage breed pig farming to motherhood. Like a modern-day Greek Agora, there is usually a collection of artists, writers, yogis and other interesting individuals sitting around her island watching her roll out biscuits while discussing life. She welcomes everyone and is known for making you laugh with her many stories.

Patricia and her husband Karl Glaeser, who has a degree in animal husbandry, bought this farm nearly five years ago. They had very little farming experience but a lot of faith. Since the purchase, they have thrown themselves into creating a sustainable, thriving farm that specializes in heritage breeds of pigs, chickens and cows. Additionally, Patricia opens her gourmet kitchen to teach cooking classes, host weddings and special events, and prepare breakfast for the bed and breakfast they run on property.

Faith Like a Mustard Seed Farm is a prime example of Pinterest envy. On the board would be a picture of her gourmet kitchen with top-of-the-line appliances and wide apron front sink. The next picture would be of her red barn and white silo sharply contrasted against the green pastures and mountains in the distance. A picture of her antique iron basket filled with an assortment of eggs in different shapes and colors would follow the barn. Her life looks beautiful and bucolic—the stuff of romantic novels. But those of us sitting around her island have talked to Glaeser enough to understand what it really means to be a farmer.

"Farming is physically demanding," she explains to the group visiting her island this morning. "But it's also really beautiful too."

Farming done well, up to the Glaeser couple's standards, requires a lot of hard work to make the quality products that Patricia truly enjoys using in her kitchen. They created a state-of-the-art hydroponic feed system so that their animals can have organic, non-GMO feed. They choose heritage animals best for free-range, small family farms. They constantly test their raw milk for contamination, and have one of the cleanest facilities around.

∧ Faith Like a Mustard Seed turkeys have free range around the farm

<< Patricia Glaeser feeds her chickens

Patricia explains that these pasture-raised farming practices allow the animals to have a happier, healthier life. These practices are also better for the environment, for the people who work on the farm, and for those who consume its products. But, this type of farming requires more time and space than the factory farms that have overtaken our food supply. This contributes to making local food much more expensive.

Similar to Sara Brown at Oakland Green Farm, Patricia Glaeser does not think food should be cheap. Some things don't seem to make sense when you look at what Americans used to spend on food compared to now. According to the United States Department of Agriculture, Americans used to spend 18 percent of their income on food in the 60s but currently spend under ten percent today. "Doesn't spending typically show where our priorities lie?" asks Patricia. "Given the nation's healthcare crisis, looking to spend more money on higher quality food seems like the right thing to do."

Even though local products may be priced higher, Glaeser claims it can be hard for farmers to make a profit, especially with the cost of land in this area. She feels that agritourism and second jobs are typically what help farmers stay afloat—in her case, the cooking classes and events are what bring in enough money to keep the farm operating.

"Where do we want to spend our money?" asks Patricia. She feels that it should be spent on things that matter like family health and by supporting local, sustainable food sources. "What do we want to share with our community—do we want to spend money on good food products or let the land be developed for more housing?"

Glaeser is passionate about her ability to provide good food and serve as a community gathering place for Western Loudoun. She feels it is important to know what talents you can share with the world, and that communities should support what they feel is important. The group of artists around her island nod enthusiastically in agreement.

At times, it feels as though this modern era is at odds with family farms. Farming takes patience, which she feels is an important lesson. She makes an example with her daughter Lauren. "There is something beautiful in making your child wait for the seasons. They learn patience and anticipation, and then there is a sweet reward," Patricia says. Communication can also be challenging in this day of instant answers. Customers have questions and are used to prompt responses, but Patricia finds it hard to answer email or text messages when she's milking cows or castrating pigs. She says that she has lost a few customers because of her inability to respond immediately, but those who are patient are rewarded as soon as they slice off a piece of amazingly moist Boston Butt or try the farm's house-made bacon.

"Life isn't supposed to be easy, it should be cherished," she says. As we bite into her ham biscuits we have watched her make for nearly an hour, a rooster softly crows in the background, and we take a moment to cherish that bite and this bucolic life we have the privilege of visiting.

<< Built in the 1840s, the farm sits on the original Lucketts Road

The farm offers a dairy share for fresh milk v

Dried Cherry Stuffed Pork Tenderloin with Roasted Potatoes and Bacon Sherry Vinaigrette

From Patricia Glaeser at Faith Like a Mustard Seed Farm
Serves 4

INGREDIENTS:

1 pound baby red potatoes

½ cup plus 2 tablespoons olive oil, divided

1 tablespoons toasted sesame oil

Fine grain sea salt and freshly ground black pepper

1 cup dried cherries

2 tablespoons minced fresh thyme leaves, divided

½ cup water

1 (20-ounce) cleaned pork tenderloin

2 tablespoons of canola or grapeseed oil

½ cup uncooked bacon chopped

½ cup finely diced red onion

1 teaspoon minced garlic

2 ½ tablespoons sherry wine vinegar

½ cup extra virgin olive oil

DIRECTIONS:

Preheat the oven to 400°F. Halve the red potatoes and toss the potatoes with the olive oil, sesame oil, and the salt and pepper. Place in a roasting pan or a sheet pan and roast in the preheated oven for 35 to 40 minutes or until slightly golden and cooked through.

Meanwhile prepare the dried cherry stuffing. Put the cherries and one tablespoon of minced thyme leaves in a medium saucepan. Add the water and bring to a simmer over medium-low heat. Simmer for five minutes, then turn off heat. Let stand for 15 minutes. Season with salt and pepper and set aside to allow to cool.

To prepare the pork tenderloin, use a sharp knife to cut a slit through the center; it should cut halfway through the depth of the tenderloin. Turn the tenderloin and cut another slit to create an X in the center. Use your fingers to help stretch a hole through the center of the X. Then, once again using your fingers, stuff as much filling as possible into the loin. Season the outside with salt and pepper.

Place a large, oven-safe sauté pan or cast iron skillet over medium heat and allow to get very hot, but not smoking. Add the canola oil and then the stuffed pork loin. Sear the loin on all sides until browned evenly. Then place the pan in the oven and roast for 25 minutes until a meat thermometer placed into the center of the pork registers at least 150°F. Remove from the oven and let rest for 10 minutes before slicing. The pork will still be a bit pink inside. If you want your pork well done, cook for an additional five minutes or so.

While the pork is in the oven, prepare the bacon sherry vinaigrette. Heat a sauté pan to medium and add the bacon. Cook for two minutes and then add the red onion and garlic. Sauté for a few minutes until the onion is translucent and the garlic is fragrant. Add the remaining tablespoon of minced thyme and cook for one more minute or until the bacon looks crispy. Transfer the pan's contents to a jar or bowl. Add the sherry wine vinegar and then slowly whisk in the olive oil and season with salt and pepper.

To serve, place a quarter of the potatoes onto a dinner plate. Slice the pork tenderloin into quarter-inch thick slices and place three slices on top of the roasted potatoes. Spoon some of the bacon and sherry vinaigrette over the pork and around the plate and season with some freshly ground black pepper. Serve and enjoy.

Life isn't supposed to be easy, it should be cherished.
– Patricia Glaeser

Buttermilk Scones with Dried Currants

From Patricia Glaeser at Faith Like a Mustard Seed Farm
Serves 18

INGREDIENTS:

4 cups all purpose flour

1 tablespoon plus 1 teaspoon
   baking powder

½ teaspoon salt

⅔ cup plus ¼ cup sugar

2 ¼ sticks Kerrygold butter

2 large eggs

1 cup buttermilk

1 tablespoon vanilla extract

1 cup dried currants

1 tablespoon orange zest

DIRECTIONS:

Position your oven rack to the center and preheat to 350°F. Line a baking sheet with parchment paper.

Put all dry ingredients into a food processor fitted with a metal blade, and pulse a few times to mix.

Add the butter to the food processor all at once, and run for 15 seconds. Switch to pulse and continue pulsing until there are no chunks of butter left, and the mixture looks like moist crumbs. Do not over-mix. Dump the mixture into a big bowl.

In a small bowl, whisk the eggs to break up the yolks. Whisk in the buttermilk and vanilla, and then stir in the currants and orange zest.

Pour the wet ingredients into the bowl with the flour mixture and stir with a wooden spoon. Even though it will be dry at first, keep mixing and it will come together. Stop mixing as soon as no flour is visible; do not work the dough any longer than necessary.

Use a half-cup measuring cup to scoop out the batter and place onto the baking sheet, leaving two inches between each scone.

Bake the scones for 25–30 minutes, until the tops are golden brown, and a toothpick inserted into the center comes out clean.

Remove the baking sheet from the oven and transfer the scones to a wire rack to rest for a few minutes. Serve fresh from the oven or at room temperature.

TARARA AND
BONEYARD WINERIES

The State of Affairs of Virginia Wine

Talking to professor-like Jordan Harris, the head winemaker at Tarara Winery in Lucketts, feels like getting a lesson in the science of winemaking, business transformation, and local policy. He knows how to make the teachings of these disciplines interesting for those who may not be particularly well-versed.

13648 Tarara Ln
Leesburg, VA 20176

tarara.com

Harris jokingly makes comments about why he decided to move from Canada to Virginia. "I'm a Rhône geek [meaning Côtes du Rhône, a wine region in France] and love that [Rhône varietal] viognier can grow in Virginia…I wanted to try my hand at it." But, then Harris gets serious when talking about the state of Virginia wine as a whole. "We can't be all things to all people," he muses, a sentiment that has been solidified during his time at Tarara. According to Harris, the state's winemakers and industry marketers, or at the very least those in Loudoun County, may want to think about changing the way they make and sell their wines.

The first grapes were planted at Tarara in 1987, and the winery and its tasting room opened two years later. Being one of the earliest wineries in Northern Virginia, it quickly became a tourist destination. Locals and visitors alike would travel to taste wines, and it wasn't uncommon for the winemakers to bottle 20 or 30 different wines each year. Some of those were flagship wines, made specifically according to the winemaker's taste, whereas many others were made for mass appeal and were a mix of fruity wines like strawberry or blackberry mixed with grape.

Harris inherited the vines at Tarara after joining the vineyard in 2007. He is the seventh winemaker on property, and spent the first couple of years undoing some previous practices. This included ripping out hybrid varieties he prefers not to grow (chambourcin, seyval, vidal) and the varietals that don't grow well at Tarara (pinot noir, pinot gris, grenache and mourvedre). He also eliminated many of the wines that were popular but not up to quality standards such as the Wild River Red blend of chambourcin and blackberry, and Cameo, a sweet rosé. "People thought I was crazy," Harris admits. "But the first thing I did when I got here was discontinue the three best selling wines. Customers told me I was nuts, but I just went after a different type of customer."

Harris ushered in a new kind of Tarara wine that placed a higher value on quality and less on the appeal to mass audiences. He also encouraged a more minimalistic winemaking style.

The winding pathway leads visitors up through the woods to the tasting room >

<< This outdoor pavilion overlooking the water is the site of a popular summer concert series

"The less I can do, the better in my opinion," he says of his approach. Harris would rather care for the terroir, or the wine-producing environment, and ensure that it is strong and healthy knowing that the soil and other environs are some of the biggest predictors in the growing success of vines and wine quality.

Harris has phased out insecticides and herbicides in recent years. Instead, he utilizes natural means to manage harmful insects, such as letting runner ducks eat pesky Japanese beetles. He also plants rows of vines closer together than many other winemakers in Virginia. He does this for a couple of reasons. First, when vines are closer, roots are forced to dig deeper into the mineral-rich layers of soil. Second, vines planted close together produce less fruit per vine, which means that less stress is placed on the vines, and this leads to more consistent soil moisture for the roots. Planting the vines closer together also allows less space for tractors and other equipment to roll over the soil, which when combined with the deeper roots, helps reduce compaction in the soil and ensures that oxygen moves down to the roots.

Harris and his team plant a 24-inch subsoil along every-other-row of grapes, which encourages the roots of vines to dig deeper for water versus growing horizontally. Deeper roots help ensure that plants survive during drought years, and likewise keeps them drier during very wet years, both of which are possible in humid Virginia. Overall, these practices lead to greater consistency.

Harris strongly believes that Virginians need to embrace the fact that great wines can be made in their home state. When asked more about this thought, he explains that many people "don't want to believe that what's in their backyard can be just as great as what is in that exotic spot on the other side of the country, but I believe 100 percent that our wines are just as good."

Harris believes that wine industry marketers need to help people understand that different wine varietals grow well in different regions across the country, and even across the state of Virginia. "I don't believe we'll be able to make as good of a cabernet sauvignon as Napa Valley can, but I don't believe there's anyone in California who can make as good of a viognier (when we get a strong yield)," Harris said. "Petit manseng, cabernet franc and merlot are far superior here. Tannatt is far superior here. [West coast winemakers] can make pinot noir and we cannot. Riesling does well in California and Washington State, but it does not grow here. Our top wines are just as good as their top wines—certainly. Just different," he continues.

One day Harris hopes that people will buy a case or two at a time from a winery here before moving onto another facility, as is the norm in wine regions throughout Europe and the west coast of the United States. Northern Virginia, and admittedly Tarara, have marketed themselves to be a place where visitors can buy one bottle at a time and sit outside and drink it for hours without buying more. While this makes for great tourism, it can hurt annual sales and growth of the industry.

According to Harris, winemakers should allow for experimentation in their practice, in addition to sticking to more traditional varietals and practices. He started a second label called The Boneyard in 2013 and uses it as his place to play and try new things without sacrificing the ideals behind Tarara's flagship labels. Inspired by a field directly outside of the vineyards that is a dumping ground for decrepit cars and tractors, Harris says that the name reminds him to embrace the past and build on it. "Look to the future in a no-rules approach" is the motto emblazoned on the bottle labels.

For the Boneyard Wines, Harris uses grapes from other wineries across the state to make varietals like a barrel-fermented rosé, a sparkling white wine made of chardonnay and a semi-orange wine (a white wine that's been fermented in its own skins). Currently, 20 percent of the 10,000 cases he bottles annually fall under the Boneyard label. He hopes to increase that in coming years and to eventually make a separate winery for it altogether.

This grower, philosopher, and scientist at work seems to constantly question how far to push the boundaries on what he can make and grow at Tarara while remaining true to the winery's roots and philosophies. One thing for sure is that Harris aims to deepen the reach of Tarara and to continue his focus on refining the quality of its wines, rather than trying to be all things to all people.

∧ The outdoor patio allows guests to enjoy the wine and the beautiful scenery

<< Tarara specializes in single vineyard blends

Strawberry, Goat Cheese and Arugula Crunch Salad

From Meghan Bollenback
Serves 8 as a side

INGREDIENTS:

¾ cup sliced raw almonds

1 ½ cups sliced strawberries

4 stalks of thinly sliced celery

7 ounces arugula, torn

4 ounces crumbled chèvre cheese

¼ cup golden or white balsamic vinegar

Juice of half a lemon

2 teaspoons honey

½ teaspoon kosher salt

¼ teaspoon freshly cracked black pepper

⅓ cup extra virgin olive oil

DIRECTIONS:

Heat a small pan over medium heat on the stove and add sliced almonds. Toast for 3 to 4 minutes, stirring a few times throughout the process. Turn off heat and set aside to cool.

While the almonds toast, slice your strawberries and celery so that the pieces are roughly ¼ to ½-inch thick.

Assemble the salad in layers by first placing half of the arugula into a large bowl or serving dish. Top with half of the strawberries, celery, almonds and chèvre. Then, repeat with the remaining amounts of each of the ingredients.

In a small bowl, combine the vinegar, lemon juice, honey, salt and pepper. Whisk to combine together. Slowly stream in olive oil and stir well to combine. Store in an airtight container in the refrigerator for up to a week.

Just a few minutes before serving, pour the dressing on top and toss lightly.

CONCLUSION

There is an open invitation awaiting you for a warm welcome to sit down over a glass of local wine or a fresh, expertly prepared meal. And while you are invited to come out and enjoy the beauty and bounty of Western Loudoun, you are also encouraged to join in the conversation about what is happening with the land out here and why.

The farmers, chefs, winemakers, brewers, and distillers are excited to engage with you about what they do and why Western Loudoun is so special. You are invited to explore each little town and village and discover their distinct personalities and identities. The places listed in this book are just to start you on your journey, because there are so many more people and places that are working to preserve Western Loudoun for you and your friends and families to continue to enjoy for generations to come.

ACKNOWLEDGEMENTS

This book would not have happened first if it were not for our immediate support system—our husbands. You both are incredible to support us in this passion project, and we love you.

Secondly, the very heart of the book—the people and their stories—happened because everyone dared to say, "Yes." when we called, emailed, or camped out inside of their stores/homes/restaurants to ask for an interview. We are in awe of those who agreed to it, and cannot thank you enough for your time, hospitality, and fervor for what you do. It is an honor to tell your stories.

Many individuals helped form our photos and rough drafts of stories into a physical product. Bonnie Bollenback (or Mom, to Meghan) proved that copyediting isn't dead and a journalism degree can indeed come in handy many years later after it was earned. Thank you so much for your many, many hours spent combing through our words and correcting all of the little things that make such a huge difference. Thank you to Art and Jenny for taking time to go through every word and acting as a safety net for details.

Lara, our amazing designer who has seemingly limitless patience, made this book what it is. Lara—your creativity, ability to synthesize our thoughts into physical layouts and design elements, and your eye for beautiful things are so impressive. We feel extremely lucky to have you as a partner on our team. Thank you for seeing our vision and making it become a gorgeous reality.

To our friends and family who believed in us enough to say, "Keep going!" when we were tempted to stop—thank you. Your supportive ideas and gentle nudges are much appreciated. Thank you to our recipe testers Annie, Amie, Andrea, Eileen, Emily, Harriet and Jeanne. Without you, we would still be in the kitchen cooking our way through the book. Thank you to Jack and Elizabeth for your constant encouragement, enthusiasm, and patience during this project.

ABOUT THE AUTHORS

Meghan Bollenback is author of the blog MegBollenback.com where she writes about her loves of food, travel, sustainability and writing. She has written for CAKE&WHISKEY, a sweet and spirited national publication that celebrates women and business, and Brazen Careerist.

Mary Litton is the author of a children's adventure series Catacombs Mysteries and currently resides in Western Loudoun. She was the Family Editor for a national online women's magazine and has written articles for national and local publications.

Photo by Joylyn Hannahs Photography

Made in the USA
Charleston, SC
17 June 2016